Evolving Creativity – new pedagogies for young children in China

Evolving Creativity – new pedagogies for young children in China

Keang-leng (Peggy) Vong

tb

Trentham Books

Stoke on Trent, UK and Sterling, USA

Trentham Books Limited
Westview House   22883 Quicksilver Drive
734 London Road   Sterling
Oakhill   VA 20166-2012
Stoke on Trent   USA
Staffordshire
England ST4 5NP

First published 2008

British Library Cataloguing-in-Publication Data
A catalogue record for this book is available from the
British Library

ISBN: 978 1 85856 404 3

Designed and typeset by Trentham Print Design Ltd., Chester and
printed in Great Britain by Cromwell Press Ltd, Wiltshire.

Contents

Acknowledgements

I would like to thank all the headteachers, teachers and children at the two kindergartens for their openness in sharing ideas with me. I am also grateful to Eve, Celia and Dennis for their continuous support and guidance during the course of this piece of exploratory work. They have made me come to terms with my Chinese identity.

My sincere gratitude for my colleagues and friends: Lai Kun, Yuk Lin, Man, Dr. Lee Appler, Dr. Dan Wei and Prof. Christopher Kelen who have shown their support for me in their special ways.

Many thanks to those who have contributed to this book, but for various reasons, I have not been able to include their names here.

I also owe Dr. Gillian Klein my deepest gratitude for her professional advice on and patience with this piece of writing.

For my late mother
Without her I simply wouldn't exist

Foreword

This book is unique yet it portrays a universal phenomenon. Its uniqueness lies in the setting, the participants and also the author herself. Of universal interest are the questions and issues that underpin the book, namely: How do individuals, especially Early Years teachers, deal with sudden immense and obligatory change? In what ways do decisions made by politicians transform teachers' and children's lives? How far can teachers retain traditional beliefs and practices yet embrace new ideas? Must initiating new ideas mean abandoning the old – or might a fusion of the best of both worlds be possible? Within these universal questions are those particular to the setting: Can educational goals and ideology move across countries and cultures? What happens when we try to transplant Western goals into a country which has different goals, traditions and values? What effects might this have on children's learning?

This is a tale of two cities and about how Early Years educators began to transform their practice whilst still retaining ownership of traditional beliefs and ideals. One of the cities is Macao, a 16 square kilometre peninsula tied to the Chinese mainland but until 1999 a Portuguese colony and the oldest European settlement in the East. Its past is still clearly evident in its Portuguese architecture, its street signs, its European feel – and the background and educational practices of some of its teachers and schools. Yet, in spite of this outer façade, most of its inhabitants are of Chinese origin and blend East and West in their cultural and educational practices. Facing Macao, and separated symbolically by an iron gate, is Zhuhai, always a mainland Chinese city, with its history of the revolution, Maoism and traditional Chinese educational goals and now part of the special economic development zone.

Both cities are part of the economic miracle that is China now, a miracle that politicians wish to enhance through the introduction of *creative curricula*, especially in the Early Years. So this is the story of how multicultural and multilingual Macao meets monolingual and monocultural Zhuhai in a quest to develop the same goals, materials and curricula. We see how two groups of teachers, coming from very different training and histories, begin to ask: What should 'count' as teaching and learning in the Early Years? How might young children's creativity best be fostered? The book traces the journey of these teachers' transformation and the effect on their children's work.

This story unfurls as the ways teachers fuse traditional and modern practices are meticulously unpicked by the author, herself a beneficiary of both Eastern and Western education and upbringing. The story told in this book resonates with experiences in Early Years education in the West and is equally important for western Early Years educators, students of comparative education and those interested in fostering creativity in all educational settings.

The author provides insights important to the West on a number of different levels. We see how teachers realise that learning new philosophies and approaches does not and should not mean sacrificing traditionally held beliefs, skills and wisdom. We see how young children blend traditional strengths of close observation and careful attention to detail with free expression to create work of quite extraordinary quality.

This is a sincere and beautifully realised book, which will sit beside studies such as those of Tobin, Wu and Davidson (1989) and appeal to all those studying education who want to broaden their knowledge of different ways of learning, being and doing. Teachers in the West have much to learn from the experiences of their colleagues in China. At a time when Early Years education in the UK is in danger of losing its autonomy to the edicts of politicians, we need to look to China to realise that our colleagues there are fighting to gain what we may well lose.

Freedom and creativity in young children cannot be taken for granted and need to be explicitly nurtured by teachers. Readers, themselves may judge the dedication of the teachers we meet in this book through the quality of the children's work. Such insights into change are unique. This is an optimistic book, looking towards an exciting future in the Chinese new world and with lessons that transcend boundaries.

Eve Gregory

Reference

Tobin, J.J., Wu, D.Y.H. and Davidson, D.H. (1989) *Pre-School in Three Cultures*, New Haven, Connecticut: Yale University Press.

Introduction

A stone gate, dated 1849, has stood solemnly at the border between Macao and mainland China for more than a hundred years. It was an emblem of Portuguese sovereignty over Macao soil, a divide for two systems of jurisdiction, a partition for two cultures and a wall for two mind sets. Today, almost nine years after the sovereignty of Macao was returned to the Chinese Government, only a few people passing by the border still pay any attention to it.

Different educational concerns on each side of the Gate

On one side of the Gate lies Macao peninsula and on the other is Zhuhai, a mainland Chinese city. These two cities reflect the cultural divide while existing in the same landscape and it is these comparisons and contrasts which make them full of interest and vigour. Living and working in Macao and providing an advisory service to a kindergarten in Zhuhai, I used to walk in and out of these cities several times a week. As a consequence, these visits provided me with opportunities to witness the differences of Macao and Zhuhai in terms of their education system, kindergarten curricula, teacher training programmes and ways of living.

As a teacher trainer in the field of Early Childhood Education in Macao (now known as Macao Special Administrative Region or Macao SAR, China), I have had opportunities, since 1995, to visit different kindergartens in Macao SAR, to talk to teachers, and to discuss issues of early childhood education in Macao SAR with headteachers. Because of my field of work, a friend of mine who owns a kindergarten in Zhuhai Special Economic Region (known as Zhuhai SER, China) asked me to supervise the programme of her kindergarten. I took on the responsibility as an opportunity to put theories of early childhood education into practice and supervised this kindergarten as a voluntary programme director from 1997 to 2003. During that period, I also communicated with parents, teachers and headteachers of other kindergartens as well as officials of the Zhuhai Education Commission.

During these activities, I was reminded of the kindergartens that I had visited when I was still a student in the US. Working as a research assistant, I had to collect data at the kindergartens and pay frequent visits to them. I was impressed then by the space and setting of the physical learning environment, the headteachers' and teachers' philosophies, as well as their conceptions of early childhood education, which to a great extent was reflected in their programmes. This understanding of the US kindergarten curricula and the philosophies that they uphold became the foundation of my knowledge of Western ideas of early childhood education. Subsequently, as a teacher trainer, I have tried to broaden this knowledge by visiting kindergartens outside Macao SAR. So far, I have been to France, Britain, Portugal, Spain, Japan, Taiwan, Hong Kong and many kindergartens in mainland China. Both intentionally and unintentionally, I have been constantly making comparisons between the kindergarten curricula in the Western world and those in Macao SAR and Zhuhai SER. In the beginning, I was comparing the physical learning environment of the kindergartens in the West, Macao SAR and Zhuhai SER. However, as the Western ideologies of early childhood education are discussed by Chinese scholars and admired by local kindergarten headteachers, teachers and government officials overseeing kindergarten in Macao SAR and China, I became interested in comparing the whole curricula and pedagogies with those in Western countries as well.

As a teacher trainer in Macao SAR, I have ample opportunities to discuss issues relating to kindergarten programmes in Macao SAR with teaching staff, who are very keen to talk about their ideas and concerns. While teachers and headteachers share similar concerns about issues such as parents' ideas of what young children should learn at kindergartens and governmental support for kindergarten resources, they also have job related concerns. Teachers find it difficult to deal with the high teacher-child ratio, heavy workload and inadequate support to implement new pedagogies. Meanwhile, most headteachers are concerned with teacher qualifications and the availability of the latest information on trends in early childhood education elsewhere in the world. Even though the focus of these concern have shifted over the years, many of these issues remain and they reflect challenges that local early childhood educators have been encountering in their daily practice. More importantly, it is quite clear that those teachers are engaging in some reflective thinking about their profession.

My experience as a voluntary programme director in a kindergarten in Zhuhai SER has given me a better all-round picture of the situation of early childhood education in there than that in Macao SAR. Even though I am a teacher trainer in Macao SAR and have opportunities to talk to both kindergarten staff and government officials, what I cannot do at will is talk to parents. In contrast, in Zhuhai SER, I was able to talk to parents and learn from them what they expected from kindergartens in general and from their curricula in particular. I have learned that their main concern is whether their children are well cared for. For instance, they are concerned with the nutritional level of the meals provided and whether or not their children get a nap after lunch. When it comes to learning, only a small number of parents would like kindergartens to allow plenty of play time for their children, while most would like kindergartens to teach their children reading, writing, and mathematics.

I once asked parents of the kindergarten I supervised to indicate, through a questionnaire, what they thought the mission of early childhood programmes should be. Most parents identified moral, cognitive, physical, social, and aesthetic development of a child as their priorities. Looking at these responses, it seems that the parents do understand that a well rounded programme is needed. In fact, these five aspects have also been conventionally considered to be the ultimate goals of education in Macao SAR, reflecting that there are some fundamental educational values in Chinese culture which is shared by residents in both cities. Nevertheless, in Macao SAR, whether or not kindergarten education can boost students' academic performance is still the main concern of many parents and practitioners. Taken together, the goals of kindergarten curricula and the pedagogy implemented in these Chinese cities have manifested the Chinese conventional ideas of kindergarten education.

Yet many early childhood educators in both Macao SAR and Zhuhai SER are recognising the importance of Western ideas of quality early childhood education that are progressive in nature and play-based, which include respect for individual differences in personality, interests and the children's role in the learning process. So it is not surprising that conventional ideas of quality early childhood education are challenged and so are kindergarten programmes. But if many parents and teachers are still holding on to traditional ideas, how should contemporary kindergartens carry out their missions and interpret their roles? Or should they take a different direction?

To summarise, it is noticeable that the progressive ideas of quality early childhood education that are advocated by many Western kindergarten programmes are not only gaining the attention of educators in Macao SAR, but also that of the Chinese government because of the Western countries' economic status. The Chinese consider Westerners innovative and creative people whose abilities are reflected by their products. These products bring the countries wealth and status in the world. As the People's Republic of China became a member of the World Trade Organisation (WTO) in the year 2001, the Chinese Government would very much like to see reforms in its educational system so that future generations will be able to compete with their Western counterparts.

To my knowledge and to judge from my own schooling in Macao SAR, most kindergartens did not pay much attention to creativity before the new millennium. Whenever I was in a kindergarten classroom in Macao SAR or Zhuhai SER, I would ask myself, are we doing enough to foster creative minds? If we take seriously the progressive ideas which underpin kindergarten education and encourage children with creative minds, what kind of young learners are we fostering? Are we doing enough to enrich the creative minds of our children? Many young children in Macao SAR and Zhuhai SER are still passive in their classrooms compared with the practice of many kindergartens in the West where children enjoy a lot of freedom and take a much more active role in learning. Nonetheless, it would be unwise to adopt totally the practice of kindergartens in the West and drop our own. Kindergarten educators in the two cities should also ask the question: in what ways should reform take place?

The purpose and organisation of the book

This book examines the notion that the meanings of learning and creativity are culture-specific. Information collected from kindergartens in Macao SAR and Zhuhai SER of China reveal that there is a strong relation between the teachers' interpretations of creativity and their ideas of learning and cognition. The reflection of these ideas about creativity, learning and cognition are influenced by the social and cultural environment of these Chinese practitioners, their own school experiences and professional training which lead to particular interpretations of creativity and learning when it comes to actual situations. The cases included in this book exemplify the ways that the Project Approach, a set of teaching strategies advocated by many North American early childhood educators and commonly used to promote learning through creative art work, is being implemented in certain parts of China. The findings show that these pedagogical strategies are not merely transplanted but are being interpreted and transformed according to the social, cultural and educational values of teachers in those cities; thus they have been developed into culturally-specific new pedagogies. Finally, the book explores the relationship between different pedagogical strategies and children's development in cognition, abilities and skills. The book thus has implications internationally.

Chapter 1 provides general information on traditional and contemporary educational ideas for kindergarten education as well as the social and educational background of Macao SAR and Zhuhai SER of China. Chapter 2 briefly outlines the conceptual changes in kindergarten education theories in China before and after the establishment of the new Chinese Government in 1949. Chapters 3 and 4 cover the theoretical perspectives of the socio-cognitive development of children and the Chinese and Western interpretations of learning and creativity so as to set the framework for further discussions and theorising. Chapters 5 and 6 describe the school cultures of the two kindergartens in the study. Chapter 7 examines the ways in which the progressive ideas of kindergarten education, and in particular the idea of promoting creativity in young children, are integrated into the Chinese contexts. Chapters 8 to 10 focus on understanding the ways in which Chinese practitioners in the two different social and cultural settings interpret children's learning, cognition and creativity as well as how these interpretations are informed by their life histories. Chapter 11 delineates the results of the transformation of a progressive pedagogy in the two Chinese kindergarten settings which appear in the form of two cultural products. The conclusion shares with practitioners, policy makers and everyone interested in studying children's creativity the suggestions drawn from the findings.

1

Educational reform and social development in two Chinese cities

With a creative mind, we could look at the map of China as a jigsaw made up of different cities, each city being represented by an irreplaceable piece. In a jigsaw, any two adjacent pieces are different in shape and design, but each is part of the big picture and are bound to have certain aspects in common. The two southern cities of China, Macao SAR and Zhuhai SER, exemplify these adjacent pieces of the Chinese territory puzzle. Even though they are neighbouring cities and share the same origin, their historical backgrounds have set them apart through their specific social systems through which their kindergarten programmes have evolved. Let us now turn to the changes pertaining kindergarten education of these two cities in the light of their socio-political contexts.

Kindergarten Education in China – Continuity and Change

Traditionally, in Chinese culture, a good education implies the possibility of becoming a government official (Lee, 1999:27). Since the availability of a government office was so limited, examinations were used to screen for qualified personnel. In contemporary mainland China, given the competition for university places, examinations are used as yardsticks. And primary school children have to take examinations in order to get a place in secondary schools famous for their university entry rates. This kind of 'examination-oriented education' 應試教育 has survived in the Chinese education system from Confucius' time (c551-c479 BC) until today, and has been criticised by many con-temporary Chinese scholars. Amongst them, Tu (1998) stated that the biggest problem with such an education was that it hindered and even destroyed children's development (also see Yang, 2002).

The Chinese educational approach has also been described as a kind of 'traditional education' 傳統教育 which is teacher-centred and implies that teachers only teach what is in books and that they decide what to teach and how to teach in a standardised fashion through one-way transmission of knowledge. Wang (2002) observed that traditional edu-cation also existed in the education systems of Europe and America around the end of the 19th century, but has lingered on in the Chinese system. Tong, Li and Li (1997) captured the changes Chinese education had been going through for the past five decades, during which there was a shift from an examination-oriented, traditional education to the pursuit of the concept of 'Quality Education' 素質教育.

In the late 1980s and early 1990s, Quality Education in mainland China emerged as the drawbacks of traditional education were recognised (Li and Guo, 1997; Tu, 1998). According to Li and Guo (1997), Quality Edu-cation refers to the kind of education that, through scientific educa-tional means, would fully realise the potential an individual is born with, increase their different ability levels, maximise the acquisition of an all-rounded and harmonious development, and produce qualified nationals for Chinese society. Some Chinese scholars interpret Quality Education as a humanistic education which pays attention to the individual learning characteristics of students. Yet others explain that Quality Education is based on the goal of enhancing the goodness and virtues of the nationals where the focus is to promote students' inspira-tion to innovate (*Zhuhai Shi Jiao Yu Yan Jiu Zhong Xin*, 2001). Moreover, the objectives of Quality Education are to enhance basic qualities such as the moral, intellectual, physical, and psychological aspects of learners (Luo, 1997). Luo illustrates the seven basic principles of Quality Education for young children that constitute a kind of child-centred learning:

■ Children should be considered as the main figure in learning, whose initiatives, creativeness and eagerness in learning should be stimulated

- Education should promote the abilities and potential in every child, and every teacher has to pay attention to their own behaviour and attitudes

- Children's physical, intellectual, moral and aesthetic development should be fostered in a balanced fashion

- Pedagogical approaches should cater for the developmental needs of children instead of rushing them through the teaching objectives designed in advance

- Teachers should recognise that there are individual differences in learning and promote children's development on the basis of their actual performance level. This principle requires teachers to be observant adults who are sensitive to children's abilities and where their zone of proximal development lies so as to design the appropriate teaching methods for the children

- Teachers should create and design opportunities and conditions to guide children to take initiatives in different learning activities so as to enrich quality of their own mind and body

- Education should focus on fostering children's creativeness and Quality Education must be implemented creatively which includes the creation and establishment of different models of Quality Education to suit different regions, conditions and children (my translation)

As indicated earlier, Tong *et al* (1997) suggested that Quality Education is needed to educate, on a large scale, Chinese nationals to be capable individuals who could accomplish the mission of constructing a modern and socialist China, but that China is still struggling to reach the nation's ideal.

Under this concept of Quality Education, the teaching objectives of early years learning have also changed. In the 1950s and 1980s, the goals for kindergarten education were based on the following key issues: to build up children's physical fitness, to develop their intellectual ability, to foster their love for the country and morality, to enrich their aesthetic sense and creativity. By the 1990s, the instilling of children's interests in science was added to the goals for kindergarten education (*Zhong Guo Xue Qian Jiao Yu Yan Jiu Hui*, 1999). However, there were no suggestions about how to implement these goals.

According to Li and Guo (1997), when the construction of a healthy economy is the task of society, the teaching objectives will rest on promoting productive human resources. Naturally, the teaching objectives will focus on unlocking the potential, intelligence, initiative and creativity of the young generation. Kindergarten education should set the foundation for children's personality so that they become people who love our world, who are independent, autonomous and cooperative, and who possess the spirit to create and the ability to actualise ideas (Zhu and Pei, 2003). Thus creativity gradually becomes an important consideration in kindergarten education in mainland China.

Since the 1980s there has been a driving force to establish Creative Education 創造教育 in mainland China. Zhao (2002) believed that the key issue is to foster in young people the spirit to create and the ability to put ideas into practice. The goal is to activate learners' initiative, let them learn creatively, and open up their potential in creativeness (Zhao, 2002). This can only be achieved through learners' active participation in creative activities, so a creative thinking style should be fostered to set the foundation, while skills and methods of creative discoveries could be provided at a later stage (Zhao, 2002). Sang (2001) similarly believed that such an education was a means to promote children to be competent people in the 21st century. He advocated that in the process of learning and problem solving, children's spirit to create and their consciousness to create could be promoted. In the process, children should also apply the skills and methods involved in creativeness in order to be brave enough to be different and endeavour to create new opinions and methods (Sang, 2001). These discussions on creative education still continue and have significance in the education arena in China today.

A document entitled the Guidelines for Kindergarten Education – Trial Version was drafted in 2001. This is recognised as a widely accepted set of suggestions towards quality kindergarten education in mainland China. The Guidelines are designed to guide kindergartens towards deepening the implementation and actualisation of Quality Education in mainland China (*You Er Jiao Yu*, 2001). The Guidelines suggest five main domains for kindergarten education: Health, Language, Sociability, Science and Arts. As the blueprint for kindergarten education for the 21st Century, the Guidelines are based on a child-centred educational concept and give specific details on the objectives, content and instructions for each of the five domains. The focus for Arts differs from the goals set in the earlier decades of traditional education, requiring that opportunities be provided for children to perform freely, to use different art forms to express themselves and comprehension of the work and imagination encouraged. Also, each child's ideas and creation deserve respect. Their unique aesthetic sense and forms of expression should be assured and accepted. The process of creating should be recognised as an important way for children to express their inner feelings and reveal what they understand. Accordingly, practising skills and standardised requirements should be avoided and teachers should give children appropriate instructions on the forms of expression and skills they need at the right time, depending on children's developmental level and needs (*You Er Jiao Yu*, 2001).

These discussions on Quality Education and the enhancing of children's creativity have spread to all Chinese cities but I focus on the scenarios of kindergarten education in Macao SAR and Zhuhai SER, giving some general information on these cities before discussing the challenges in kindergarten education itself.

Transitions and changes – Macao SAR

In Macao, or Macau in Portuguese spelling, in the south of Guangdong Province, south European culture has blended into the life of the Chinese for many years. This makes it a unique place in the East.

Macao SAR is comprised of a small peninsula and two offshore islands, Taipa and Coloane, located on the south coast of Guangdong Province and connected to mainland China via Zhuhai SER. The Gate acts as a border separating the two groups of Chinese, each with their lifestyles, social values, practices and ideologies. Since the 1980s, the population remained steady after an influx of immigrants from mainland China, although numbers have gone up in recent years. The majority of Macao SAR residents are Chinese (93%) while 0.6 per cent are Portuguese and 6.4 per cent others (Macao Special Administrative Region Statistics and

Census Service, 2006). Many Macao people visit Zhuhai SER frequently for leisure activities and some even live in Zhuhai SER and work in Macao SAR, or vice versa.

Macao SAR is known for its embrace of both Western and Eastern cultures, and the Chinese and Portuguese have lived peacefully together, combining the two cultures to create the Luso-Chinês culture. The Macao SAR Government and most inhabitants would like to preserve this special character of Macao SAR because even though the majority of Macao people are Chinese, their lifestyles are somewhat westernised. People visit bars, wear brand names from France, Italy, Japan, America and other countries. Most young people call each other by their English names, and love fast food and Western music. However, Chinese moral and value systems are still preserved and both Chinese and Western festivals are celebrated. There are many European style buildings such as churches which serve all Macao residents. Living conditions are harmonious.

Historical background

The Portuguese first landed in Macao in 1553 (Jiang, 1999). They rented Macao from China for some years, then seized it from the Chinese Government and made it one of their colonies (Liu, 1999). Then on 20 December 1999, Macao was handed over to China and renamed Macao SAR, China, so ending Macao's colonial period. The One Country, Two Systems Policy 一國兩制, safeguards the stability of the transition period but even though Macao SAR has been handed over to China, it is run under the leadership of the Chief Administrator of Macao SAR. The Central Government in China, therefore, rules Macao SAR indirectly through the special administrative regional government.

Macao SAR has enjoyed two cultures for over 400 years. The influence of Portuguese sovereignty was obvious and profound, in spite of the large Chinese majority. From cobbled roads to buildings, from pace of life to cuisine, from language to garbage cans, all reflect the remains of a Portuguese colony. Portuguese culture has been absorbed into the daily life of the people. An obvious and important Portuguese influence on Macao SAR is its language. Before the handover, the official language was Portuguese. But, ironically, only a small percentage of the population understands the language well enough to even complete a government

6

form. The Portuguese government made no effort to promote Portuguese so it scarcely featured in the education system. As photo 1 shows, Portuguese and Chinese have been used alongside each other that since the handover, Chinese has become the dominant language in Macao.

Photo 1: The top one is an old street sign and Chinese characters are on the side whereas the bottom one is new and Chinese characters come first.

Transitions and changes – Zhuhai SER, China

Zhuhai SER, although a neighbouring city, has a different history and socio-cultural character. It too is situated on the southern coast of the Guangdong Province. According to the Zhuhai Special Zone Daily (2001), in the 5th census of Zhuhai SER of 2000 the population was estimated at 1.2 million. The annual increase in population is thought to be lower than the statistics obtained at the 4th census for 1980 to 1990, suggesting that the One-Child Policy has been rather effective in controlling the birth rate. The city has about 0.3 million families, constituting 0.94 million people, or 76 per cent of the population, but the family sizes have shrunk from 3.8 per family in 1990 to 3.08 today. This might suggest that the number of extended families has been diminishing whereas in fact the number of one-child families 獨生子女家庭 gone up.

Although Zhuhai SER is one of China's special economic regions, every-day life is similar to that in other mainland cities. Before 1979, the mainland Chinese demographic movements were strictly monitored, so there was little exchange between the Chinese and people in other countries and thus little cultural exchange. Even in recent years, Zhuhai SER is essentially a single culture city and the lifestyle of its people has not been drastically influenced by other cultures.

Historical background

The economy of Zhuhai is tied to its political status. It was a fishing village until 1953, when the National Affairs Office 國務院 decided that it should be developed as a county. In 1979, the Community Party planned strategically for economic reforms and the Open Door Policy of opening its markets to the world. The Central Government decided to turn Zhuhai County into a city, so in 1980 it became one of four Special Economic Regions (SER) of China benefiting from privileges granted by Central Government. Its economy accelerated at an un-precedented rate and prosperity brought social changes and problems. An influx of people from poor areas of China has increased pressure on its educational institutions and the number of kindergartens rose.

Challenges for the kindergartens in the two cities

We have seen how kindergarten education in China has changed over the years and how creativity is gradually becoming important. It goes without saying that the government kindergartens in Macao SAR and Zhuhai SER, as in other cities in China, have to observe the need for educational reform as specified by the central and local governments. The question is how the kindergarten teachers will try to meet the expectations of their respective governments.

Parents and teachers have experienced traditional ways of learning so teacher education has not prepared teachers to promote creative abilities in children. This book attempts to answer the following questions:

- Since educational aims such as creativity, problem solving and critical thinking originate from Western countries, can creativity in early childhood education be transplanted when those engaged in the process have very different understandings of what creativity means?

- How is creativity defined and interpreted in different types of schools?

- Can educational goals and ideologies move across countries and cultures? What happens when we try to transplant Western goals into a country with very different goals, traditions and values?

- How do Chinese educators go about adopting ideas from Western literature to make them their own?

- What effect does the transformed or new pedagogy have on children in the two socio-cultural contexts?

2

The background to kindergarten education in old and new China

C hina has a long history but the new China only began in 1949. In this chapter we examine the development of the concept of kindergarten education in China before and after the new China was established.

Adopting theories from the Western world before 1949

China is renowned for the value it has placed on education since Confucius' time, but the significance of early education for an individual's development was only recognised in the 20th century. Historically, the Chinese education system focused on two levels: elementary education for 7 to 15 year olds, and higher education for those over 15 (Bai, 2000). Younger children had no institutional education unless they had private tutors (Bai, 2000:139) and kindergarten education evolved from foreign educational ideas.

According to the Chinese concept of childhood, children under 7 years old were considered young and ignorant (Xu, 1977, cited in Bai, 2000), so not until the late Qing Dynasty (the early 1900s) was there thought for their education. Studies of Japanese language and Japanese translations of Western works about issues in education resulted in a decree in 1902 that children under 7 should attend institutions called, from the Japanese, *mengyangyuan* (*meng* means ignorant, *yang* means nurture, *yuan* means court – a court for nurturing the ignorant) (Bai, 2000). Their curricula resembled that of primary schools and subjects taught included recognition of Chinese characters, writing characters, the study of Confucian Classics, history, geography, gymnastics and, in the third year, mathematics (Bai, 2000).

According to the work of Li, Qi and Qian (1995), which was based on primary sources such as contemporary government documents, there were several catalysts for the establishment of the first kindergarten. The late 1800s marked the Meiji Period for Japan and the Qing Dynasty for China. Meiji Japan was affluent and advanced in technology, and Western modern weapons greatly impressed the Qing people. Chinese scholars and Government officials admired Japanese and Western wealth and modern technology.

A document in 1903 regulating the operation and staffing of *mengyang-yuans* (Li *et al*, 1995) ultimately led to the first public kindergarten, the Hubei Kindergarten or Hubei *Youzhiyuan* (*you* means young, *zhi* means naive, *yuan* means garden), opened that year. Teachers who returned from training in Japan set up normal schools for teacher training programmes (Bai, 2000). The Hubei Kindergarten was based on the Japanese curriculum, which emphasised games, play, and learning through the five senses (Shu, 1981), and it served children aged 3 to 7. So it was the Japanese interpretation of the Western educational system and the Japanese kindergarten curriculum that brought the Chinese into contact with Froebel's ideas of kindergarten education.

The awakening

In the following years, several social reforms took place. The famous Self-strengthening Movement created a new scenario for kindergartens in China as it gave women new social status. Missionaries in China actively promoted female education, opening schools for girls and women and stressing its importance. The status of kindergartens in China was still vague and neglected but by 1912, kindergartens became 'regarded as an education entity instead of as an affiliated part of charitable institutions' (Bai, 2000:152).

In 1919, the Qing Government began to reject the Japanese models because of Japan's aggression towards China. Instead, Chinese scholars began to learn directly from Western education, and the ideas of Pesta-lozzi, Froebel, Montessori and Dewey received special attention (Bai,

2000). Visits by Dewey and several other American educators to China exposed the need for reform of the kindergarten curriculum. In 1922, a decree which hugely affected the education system recognised the kindergarten as an independent institute which should be regarded as 'the first stage of a universal education' (Bai, 2000:154). Kindergartens were to admit children under 6 years old. Scholars and researchers who returned to mainland China from America in the 1930s (Bai, 2000) were key figures in this reform.

These scholars and researchers realised that the blind adoption of any Western model was problematic and were determined to establish authentic Chinese kindergartens (Bai, 2000). One scholar, Heqin Chen, who was a student of Dewey and had a Masters Degree from Columbia University Teachers' College, stressed the value of hands-on activities. He suggested that children should learn from doing, but also progress from doing. He proposed that the kindergarten curriculum should be based on nature and one's society. While the strengths of Western education should be learned, kindergarten education should suit the circumstances of mainland China. But how to adapt Western educational ideology appropriately remained unclear.

The influence of Western educational theories and pedagogies after 1949

The Qing Dynasty was superseded by the new Chinese Government in 1949 but foreign educational ideas continued to influence kindergarten education. By the 1950s, China had established its relationship with the Soviet Union. Goods, knowledge in advanced technology, and educational ideas were exchanged and Chinese scholars began learning about the Russian model of education, including kindergarten (Bai, 2000). However, the political situation in China had not calmed down, and kindergarten education was not a priority.

After political stability was regained in 1979, the kindergarten section of education departments was revived at national, provincial, and municipal levels. Various official documents and teachers' handbooks were produced and research groups interested in kindergarten education became active (Bai, 2000).

During the 1980s, the Chinese education system continued to be influenced by the theories of Dewey, Bruner, Montesorri, Piaget and Vygotsky, but also the educational ideas of Chinese scholars such as Heqin Chen and Xinzhi Tao (a student of Dewey) were revived (Li *et al*, 1995). These theories still influence kindergarten education today, as can be seen in many cities. Some programmes are based on Dewey's idea that learning means doing. There are Montessori kindergartens and others which hold to Piaget's theory of constructivism. Interest in Vygotsky's socio-cognitive development of learning is growing. Vygotsky's 'zone of proximal development' (discussed in Chapter 3) has been incorporated into the principles of Quality Education. American scholar Howard Gardner's Multiple Intelligences theory, which sees children as individuals possessing different kinds of intelligence which deserve attention in their own right, is being widely discussed and implemented in kindergartens.

The importation of Western pedagogical models into Macao SAR and Zhuhai SER

Since the 1980s Western pedagogical models and teaching methods have been widely practised in Zhuhai SER and Macao SAR. The Open Door Policy enabled kindergarten educators to exchange educational ideas and pedagogical strategies with Western colleagues. In Macao SAR, public kindergartens adapted to the Portuguese approach, whereas private kindergartens run by religious groups experimented with different pedagogies. The pedagogical models and teaching strategies that inform the teaching approaches of kindergarten practitioners in these two southern cities fall into several categories.

The Thematic Approach – A conceptual change in curriculum design

This pedagogical model was meant to replace the conventional curriculum. Traditionally, the subject areas considered important for children to acquire were separated into discrete disciplines. In contrast, the thematic approach sets a theme as the centre of learning and the subject areas or disciplines are then related around it. It has been claimed that children can thus make better sense of what has been taught and learned. Still pre-planned and structured by teachers, the teaching objectives and content have to be linked around a topic of study. The process of reorganising subject matter into themes required teachers in both cities to gradually modify the conventional curricula and teaching approaches which had been practised for many years. However, pedagogical strategies remained primarily teacher-centred.

Activity-based Approach – A learning-through-activity strategy

This approach encourages teachers to let children take initiatives in activities and discussions in order to demonstrate the expected performance and attitude. Through the knowledge they have acquired or explored by themselves, children construct their knowledge together with past experiences and motivation in learning. The key features of the activity-based approach are:

- children's individual differences are noted

- children's interests are regarded as the starting point of activities

- the learning environment is arranged to facilitate the learning activities.

The activity-based approach facilitates the acquisition of knowledge through lively learning activities that allow for children's involvement and welcomes their participation in the teaching and learning processes. It appears hand in hand with the thematic approach in many kindergartens in Macao SAR and Zhuhai SER to this day. The children are gradually given a role in their learning and more their interests are respected (*Jiao Yu Ji Qing Nian Ju Ke Cheng Gai Ge Gong Zuo Zu*, 1999).

The Project Approach – A child-centred teaching strategy

Dahlberg, Moss and Pence (2000) described Reggio Emilia as an influential and postmodern pedagogical model for early childhood education. Loris Malaguzzi, the founder of the Reggio Emilia system, believes strongly that 'our image of the child is rich in potential, strong, powerful, competent and, most of all, connected to adults and other children' (Malaguzzi, 1993:10). He emphasised the value of the relationship between child and adult and between child and child. Recognising children's capabilities and their relationship with others allowed for the co-construction of learning activities, and of knowledge, self-identity and culture (Dahlberg *et al*, 2000:50). The strong focus on developing the sense of citizenship in the town's young citizens makes it unique (Dahlberg *et al*, 1999; Edwards *et al*, 1998). The Reggio kindergartens emphasise providing lively learning experiences that allow children to express their ideas in different ways which can be observed through the ethos of 'the hundred languages of children' (how they express themselves) (Edwards *et al*, 1998). Embedded in this philosophy is that:

- children need to use different materials and different methods to represent their thoughts and ideas

- children's development depends greatly on the 'hundred languages' to allow for different ways of expressing, communicating and knowledge construction

- all the languages relate to and develop from children's lived experiences.

Most of the learning activities are in project form. The programmes are known for their artistic components and these are represented by the physical settings, the play-based learning activities and the children's art work. The Project Approach is a set of pedagogical strategies, renowned for fostering children's independent thinking and expression of creative ideas through art work activities chosen by children or by children and their teachers. The teachers used their understanding of the children's abilities and past experiences to integrate their interests and needs to design flexible and hypothetical plans for the teaching and learning events.

Chard (2001) defined the Project Approach as

> a set of teaching strategies which enable teachers to guide children through in-depth studies of real world topics. The Project Approach is not unstructured. There is a complex but flexible framework with features that characterise the teaching-learning interaction. (para 2)

The involvement of children in designing project work in schools has gained increasing attention (Katz, 1997). Applying the Project Approach to the Reggio Emilia System promoted its value. It was not meant to replace the curriculum for Early Childhood Education (Katz, 1997) but to be an important part of the curriculum, allowing children to acquire knowledge and concepts through various activities stemming from a project. Topics, and later subtopics, could be studied in small groups, while everyone was actually working towards the goal of the whole class

(Katz and Chard, 1998). Criteria for selecting project topics which would have potential interest to the children and their daily lives were defined (1998:3). The teaching objectives for the topic selected are initially planned, but as the children and teachers progress, the plan is adjusted to accommodate children's interests, needs and curiosity.

The Project Approach can cater for the developmental needs of children while providing opportunities for social activities, thus incorporating them into society (Zhu, 2000; Katz and Chard, 1998). Teaching and learning aims to be an interactive process (Chard, 2000), during which teachers and children jointly discuss and plan for the activities to be worked on, sometimes involving parents and adults in the community. Children have opportunities to reflect on their work and improve it but the results are no more important than the process itself, as cognitive challenges are invoked during the discussions and reflection phases.

The Project Approach usefully bridges the gap between a child as 'self' and their outside world. It values children's participation and independent thinking in the process of learning and the teachers have to respect their interests and ideas. It is the process rather than the end product which is valued. Project work involves the children's ideas and the varied materials are used for art work activities to promote children's imagination and creativity.

This approach poses new challenges for teachers as teaching objectives and activities are not pre-planned and structured but based on a loose framework. It recognises the significance of relationships and sees children as individuals full of potential and possibilities. This has pushed teachers in Macao SAR and Zhuhai SER to think further about their and the children's role in the pedagogy.

Conceptual changes

These teaching approaches and pedagogical models reflect progressive ideas of a child-centred, liberal, innovative, exploratory and pragmatic education (Gardner, 1989). They have brought dramatic changes to kindergarten education since the 1980s. During the last decade, the Reggio Emilia educational model and the project teaching strategy have gained increasing popularity and are being discussed and integrated into the curricula by numerous kindergartens.

One obvious consequence is that teachers are encouraging children to take a more active role in their classroom learning and modifying their teacher-centred approach. The extent of these changes varies from kindergarten to kindergarten and differs in the two cities featured in this book. Pedagogical models and teaching strategies have always originated outside Macao SAR and Zhuhai SER. So teachers are periodically given opportunities to learn from pedagogies which are based on the beliefs and values of other cultures. The next chapter examines the key theories on children's cognitive development, the different interpretations of creativity and links them with Chinese kindergarten practices.

3

Linking culture, creativity and pedagogical approaches

Historically, researchers interested in children's cognition and learning studied these aspects as if they were independent of the individual's social environment (Cole and Scribner, 1977; Cole, 1985). Swiss psychologist Jean Piaget and his followers maintain that thought processes and the formation of cognitive structures are the result of interactions between the individual and the physical environment. The structural approach generated a large volume of research in European countries and the US.

However, as the methodological issues and difficulties of research on cognitive processes are widely discussed and acknowledged and cross-cultural studies escalate (for example: Mead, 1964; Wertsch, Rio and Alvarez, 1995; Rogoff, 1990; Rogoff *et al*, 1993), there is substantial evidence that an individual's thought processes are closely related to their socio-cultural environment. This line of research argues that human cognition and development are strongly linked to or influenced by the cultural contexts in which one resides, forming the underlying ideology of social cognitive psychology. As Jerome Bruner stated: 'Theories of human development, once accepted into the prevailing culture, no longer operate simply as descriptions of human nature and its growth' (1986: 134).

The discussions and cross-cultural research on the relationship between the individual's cultural context and social environment, and their development have received increasing attention. Research exploring the interrelationship between children's social worlds, cognitive development and learning has pedagogical implications for educators (Luria, 1976; Rogoff, 1984; Cole, 1990 and 1998). The social aspects of cognition appear to have drawn people's attention to the mechanism of social influence and challenged the Piagetian model.

Russian psychologist and educator Lev S Vygotsky was probably the most prominent figure in the study of the relation between cognition and culture. He was the first scholar to suggest the mechanisms by which culture becomes part of each person's nature (Wertsch, 1985:7). Vygotsky believed that cognitive development should be considered as a process of acquiring culture, and that cognitive processes were actually 'internalised transformations of socially prevalent patterns of interpersonal interactions' (Cole, 1985:148). Vygotsky and his students termed this approach a 'socio-cultural' or 'socio-historical' theory of psychological processes (Cole, 1985:148). Human psychological processes appeared on the social and individual level, ie 'first, between people (interpsychological) and then inside the child (intrapsychological) ... All these higher functions originate as actual relations between human individuals' (Vygotsky, 1978:57).

One of the notions stemming from Vygotsky's framework of socio-cultural or sociohistorical phenomena is the zone of proximal development or ZPD. Vygotsky defined ZPD as 'the distance between the actual developmental level as determined by independent problem solving and the level of potential development as determined through problem solving under adult guidance or in collaboration with more capable peers' (Vygotsky, 1978:86). The application of the ZPD to how an inexperienced person advances in learning with adult assistance and guidance can be observed in different social contexts.

Socio-cultural views of development and Chinese pedagogical approaches

The Chinese culture is a collectivistic one which focuses on interpersonal relationships amongst people in the same society rather than individualistic ideas of self and the group (Triandis, 1989). Children growing up in a collectivistic society such as China are likely to be influenced by their social interactions. The socio-cultural theory characterised by the ZPD approach is useful in explaining the pedagogy observed in Chinese classrooms where adult assistance and guidance are important to children's learning.

Also linking the Vygotskian model to the Chinese classroom practices is the theory that children's development and learning are embedded in various social worlds –

- the adults' world outside the school context (Childs and Greenfield, 1982; Lave, 1978)

- the adults' world within the school system (Brown and Ferrara, 1985; Daniels, 2001; Hedegaard, 1990; Tharp and Gallimore, 1988; Bodrovo and Leong, 1996)

- a world with adults as their learning partners (Stone, 1987; Rogoff, 1990; Rogoff and Gardner, 1984)

- a world in which peers become co-learners (Brownell and Carriger, 1998; Rogoff, 1990; Tudge, 1989; Forman and Cazden, 1985; Baker-Sennett, Matusov and Rogoff, 1992)

As they take part in social interactions and activities within these social groups, children benefit in different ways. In Western cultures, it might seem irrelevant to mention the importance of the influence each social group has on young children. But in the Chinese tradition, where social hierarchy is structural and fairly rigid, adults and especially teachers play a crucial role in children's learning and cognitive development. From caring and teaching to disciplining, teachers are expected by parents and others in the social system to set high standards for academic achievement and conduct (Chao, 1994). Shouldering these responsibilities, Chinese teachers' teaching style is often regarded as strict and even harsh. Authoritarian as they may seem, authoritarianism in Chinese terms also implies responsibility, concern, guidance, etc (Chao, 1994). In Chinese teachers' pedagogy the adults' approach is determined by the goal of development, values and practice they consider important in their culture.

In the late 1980s, Tobin, Wu and Davidson illustrated how the teachers at kindergartens in three cultures differed in their views of early year education and practice. Almost 10 years later, Cook (1999) described how the Islamic culture was influenced by Western educational ideologies and in what ways these influences were reflected in Islamic peda-gogies. These studies illustrate that the implementation of children's learning activities and pedagogies by teachers are closely related to their cultural views of education. The cultural perspectives of education are often reflected through the pedagogical models and approaches the teachers adopt.

A teacher-centred approach is still practised and student compliance is still expected (Ho, 2001). Headteachers and teachers determine the educational goals, philosophy of teaching and learning, and the values attached to their pedagogy. They determine the classroom activities and learning characteristics pertaining to those activities. The peda-gogy observed is teacher-centred: seldom do children play a part in choosing the subject matter being taught or the classroom activities. Ho argued that the student-centred orientation in the West might even 'appear irrelevant in the training of Asian teachers' (2001: 99). However, another education reform which pushes for creativity-based curricula and pedagogies is in full force, changing the pedagogies employed in kindergarten classrooms.

Early years learning in China

Wollons (2000) and Tobin *et al* (1989) looked at kindergarten pro-grammes in Japan, England, Australia, America, China, Germany, Poland and elsewhere. Their work reveals that there is more than one pedagogical approach and that each functions within a unique cultural context. The differences in pedagogical approaches might be narrowed through exchanges of educational ideologies but the impact certainly varies from case to case, as an account of the scenario in China illus-trates.

Most theories studied by Chinese early childhood educators were im-ported from countries with a different culture (Chen, 1996). Even today, written works by Froebel, Dewey, Montessori and Piaget are influential. Huo (1995) argued that learning from the experiences and early child-hood ideologies of other countries can help mainland China see the strengths in others and the weaknesses in herself.

However, Chen was concerned about Chinese kindergarten teachers' mastery of these concepts as many of them mistakenly believe that if the child is the main figure in learning, they need not be disciplined. But although the child-centred approach views the child as the main figure in learning, there must also be recognition of the important role the teacher plays in the process to 'induce initiative out of the child' (Pan, 1993:92). Accordingly, activities organised in the classrooms are classified into play and games, routines and learning activities. Play games and routines are accomplished through role-play, physical exercise, imitation of behaviour and inner experiences in which learning takes place randomly and is only situational. But learning activities are purposeful, planned intellectual activities based on the basic characteristics of cognitive styles and are therefore essential means of learning (Pan, 1993).

As early as the 1930s, Heqin Chen (see Chapter 2) attempted to adapt Dewey's education ideology in early childhood education in China. Chen established the first private kindergarten in Jiansu Province, where he experimented with theories of child psychology and early childhood education and designed his own curriculum and teaching materials (He, 1988). Chen proposed the idea: learn through doing, teach through doing and process through doing. He believed that as long as children do things with their hands, their minds are working. Noticing that Western education ideologies were applied without critical thinking, Chen stressed that kindergarten education should be designed in a way suited to the special circumstances of mainland China. He (1988: 84) quoted Chen's view of teaching Chinese children how to draw:

> ... pictures should be drawn by oneself, but it takes guidance. If a child draws by himself casually, without teachers' guidance, he cannot draw good pictures ... But how to guide them? I have several methods: one is by demonstration, one is by correction ...

Xinzhi Tao was a student of Dewey and an influential educator in mainland China at the same time. He shared a similar ideology to Chen about early years learning and advocated the need for creative education in China. Tao proposed that life is education, society is school, and that teach, learn and do are all united. In contemporary times, Zhu and Pei (2003) have reviewed the socio-cultural or socio-historical view of cognitive development and interpreted the teaching and learning process as the shifting of responsibility from adult to child. For them, scaffolding works in the following manner:

> At the beginning, the adult's responsibility is to provide the child with complex interference and lots of scaffolds, give the child guidance which include demonstrating the correct way of doing things, remind them not to forget, simplify the steps in the problem so that the child can handle them, maintain a child's interest in the task, state the discrepancies between the actual action and the desired action, monitor frustration level, show the child the ideal state of the on-going action, etc. (Zhu and Pei, 2003:6)

Zhu and Pei believed that the Vygotskian view of learning has inspired many early childhood educators to rethink difficult issues regarding the relationship between teaching, learning and development. There has been a strong emphasis on the sensibility of the adults involved in the teaching and learning process which will benefit children's cognitive development. Teachers should offer timely assistance, support or guidance and not leave children to learn on their own; nor should they jump too quickly into the situation and overwhelm them with instructions.

Pedagogical positions in early years learning

Although imported educational ideas have been discussed in mainland China, indigenous ideas of education are still in place. For instance, in a book prepared for kindergarten teacher training programmes, Wu stresses that 'practice makes perfect' in the learning process and that knowledge is established by repeating the task. Taking drawing as an example, Wu emphasises the skills and techniques involved in drawing, for example: 'without mastering the lines, shades, use of colours, and other key knowledge about drawing; without witnessing how others draw; there is no way to master the skills in drawing' (Wu, 1993:108). He believes that if you have knowledge of drawing but do not do it with your own hands and do not practise, the skills will not be developed. Skills and abilities are different concepts, in that acquired knowledge cannot be directly transformed into ability. Only after the knowledge is applied in practice and through the formation of skills is ability developed (Wu, 1993). So basic knowledge and basic skills are equally important in early years learning.

Various interpretations of early years learning, whether imported or indigenous, emerged at different times. While the child gradually comes to be seen as the main figure in the teaching and learning process, the teacher's directing role is still emphasised. While the benefits of early experiences with the environment are valued, the teacher's role in guiding through demonstrations and correction of mistakes is stressed. Even though it is advocated that education should be based on children's initiatives and interests, many Chinese educators still prioritise the transmission of skills, acquisition of techniques and basic knowledge.

Fitting creativity within views of early years learning

The importance of fostering creativity in children is clear in government documents and academic literature of both Western and Asian countries. It is regarded today as a vital human capacity for future generations, who will be living in a fast changing, unpredictable and competitive world (Craft, 2002; Wang *et al*, 1998). The issue of creativity has brought teaching objectives under revision (eg in the *NACCCE Report* (1999), in Britain and The Guidance for Kindergarten Education – Trial Version, in China) and the revised objectives inform early childhood practitioners of what children are to learn. The emphasis of the guiding documents on fostering creativity in children stems from economic concerns in China which make it imperative to develop new pedagogy. Yet researchers argued that attention to the 'what' of learning does not mean much without understanding the 'how' (Anning and Edwards, 1999).

Cognition, knowledge or behaviour change during the process of learning (Runco, 1996). Creativity is a human capacity which, like other abilities can be fostered in young children (Maynard, 1973; Duffy, 1998). But what creativity means to people varies according to the society or culture. So do their notions of how learning takes place and the strategies they employ to foster creativity. The differences are complicated still further when a concept or pedagogical strategies are transplanted from one culture to another.

Western interpretations of creativity: still an on-going process

Before Chinese scholars borrow the ideas of creative education and such pedagogy from the West, they have to have a good grasp of what their Western counterparts mean by creativity. However, Western literature yields no agreed definition of creativity. Craft (2002) sketched a historical picture of initial explorations of creativity dating back to Greek, Judaic, Christian and Muslim traditions. All these cultures used the notion of 'inspiration' to explain the human capacity, 'to develop new ideas and original products' (p1). Fluency, flexibility and originality were seen as significant factors in creative behaviour (Guilford, 1967, cited in Craft, 2002). For Fredelle Maynard (1973) creativity was something new – the opposite of copying or imitating. It involved a genuine expression of self, a special kind of perception, a capacity for absorption when completing a task of interest, willingness to take risks, and it was non-conformative. Creative people were 'curious, flexible, inventive, spontaneous, playful, observant and free' (Maynard, 1973:12). His view of creativity focused on the individual and their independent thinking.

On the other hand, Howard Gardner (1989) saw creativity as the capacity 'to solve problems or to fashion products in a domain, in a way that is initially novel but ultimately acceptable in a culture' (p14). Creativity is not a trait like intelligence, which 'individuals possess to greater or lesser extent and which can be applied equally to any content' (p113). Rather, 'there are many varieties of creativity, each restricted to a particular domain ... Mozart could not have been a great physicist, Newton a world class musician' (p112). Gardner argues for 'recognition of the fact that most human accomplishment is domain-specific and cannot be expected to be found across disparate areas of expertise' (p114). But creative people often have creative ideas and make creative products, although these might not be recognised as creative at the time they are produced. Some, however, are accepted in time.

Mihaly Csiksentmihalyi similarly defined creativity as 'the process in which a cultural symbolic domain is changed. New songs, new ideas, new machines are all related to creativity' (1996:18). Csiksentmihalyi claimed that for something to be considered creative, it has to add value to one's culture: it must receive social recognition and survive evaluation by experts. He emphasises the immeasurable and unprecedented achievements: creative individuals like Picasso, Thomas Eddison, Einstein and Leonardo de Vinci, who have significant ideas that change our cultures and the history of humankind. This, for Csiksentmihalyi, is the creativity of genius.

Sternberg and Lubart (1995) focused on the notion of the creative product. This has two essential elements: novelty and appropriateness – the product must be an appropriate answer to some question. They define a novel product as 'original, not predictable', and as something that 'can provoke surprise in the viewer because it is more than the next logical step ... that is novel but doesn't fit the constraints of the problem at hand is not creative...' (p12). High quality products show excellent technical skills and offer the possibility of different ways of implementation. The product's quality depends also on the scope of the idea and how much it influences the ideas of others.

Anna Craft developed Roger and Maslow's interpretation of creativity as self-actualisation to distinguish 'big C' creativity and 'little c' creativity. 'Big C' creativity is possessed by a few creative minds, whereas 'little c' creativity exists in ordinary people and implies 'the resourcefulness and agency of ordinary people. Like Csiksentmahalyi, Craft believes that there is 'a recognition of the kind of creativity that actually changes the domain' (Craft, 2002:52)

> It is the sort of creativity, or 'agency', which guides route-finding and choices in everyday life. It involves being imaginative, being original/ innovative, stepping at times outside of convention, going beyond the obvious, being self-aware of all of this in taking active, conscious, and intentional action in the world. It is not, necessarily, linked to a product-outcome. (Craft, 2002: 56)

Craft draws parallels between 'little c' creativity and the notion of 'democratic' creativity described in the NACCCE Report. A democratic perspective connotes that everyone is creative in some areas and everyone should be given equal opportunities to stretch their potential (NACCCE Report, 1999:29). To meet the economic, technological, social and personal challenges imposed on this and future generations, it is necessary to realise and promote the creativeness of all young people, whatever their domain of talent. Creative and cultural education should imbue the foundation years. Creativity is defined as having four features: imagination, purpose, originality and value: it is any 'imaginative activity fashioned so as to produce outcomes that are both original and of value' (*NACCCE Report*, 1999: 30).

This review of research into creativity is far from exhaustive. It reveals the problem of trying to define this term: there is clearly no adequate definition or ultimate consensus. Early attempts focus on the individual's independent thinking and pay little attention to the social aspects of ideas. Certain criteria for creativity seem to ignore the creativity children show in their ideas about products, although this may not match the characteristics of creativity identified by Csiksentmihalyi and Gardner. Craft's theory of 'big C' and 'little c' creativity suggests different levels of creativity and encompasses the development of small children's natural and ordinary 'little c' which might even have a spark of genius. That the perspectives of creativity are so different may be because they lie within different philosophical positions and cultural frameworks. Each interpretation is produced for a different purpose, thus affecting the meaning of a concept. Ultimately, children's creativity has not received enough attention, nor has it been fully understood.

Amongst the various interpretations of creativity it is agreed that originality is a feature. And the outcomes produced must fulfill a purpose or solve a problem. Three possible dimensions of creativity are evident. Firstly, social recognition and cultural aspects are embedded in it. Secondly, it covers wider human abilities than just artistic expression. Thirdly, imagination is a pre-requisite. However, as Ken Robinson wrote about the efforts to define creativity, 'the problems lie in its particular associations with the arts, in the complex nature of creative activity itself, and in the variety of theories that have been developed to explain it' (*NACCCE Report*, 1999:28).

The Chinese interpretation of creativity: still not resolved

Though based on the many Western views of creativity, the Chinese interpretation of creativity is yet more complicated. Viewed from a Eastern perspective, the various definitions of creativity not only carry Western tones but also reflect Chinese ideas of education and learning.

Wang *et al* (1998) suggested that even though China was once famous for her discoveries, the ability to create did not gain enough attention and the literature which records ancient Chinese creation and dis-coveries is sparse. Only in the 1940s did the eminent Chinese scholar Xinzhi Tao draw attention to the importance of fostering creativity in young people (also see Dong, 1995:60) but it was not until the Open Door Policy was enforced that scholars in China revived Tao's ideas about creativity. In the early 1990s, they translated Western theories and studies about creativity (Dong, 1995) and by the mid 1990s, studies on creativity at different levels proliferated (Wang *et al*, 1998).

Two Chinese characters make up the word 'create': 創造 (*Chuang Zhao*). These imply 'making' or 'producing' for the first time. According to the Chinese dictionary《辭源》(*Ci Yuan*) (1951;1980), when it was first used, the character 創 (*Chuang*) could by itself mean 'the first' (or the beginning) and 'the making of' (or producing). These meanings can be traced back to the Spring and Autumn Period (722 BC – 480 BC) during which Confucius had used the term in the Analects (《論語》) (also see Wang *et al*, 1998:16). But the term creativity does not appear in the 1951 edition of the Chinese dictionary.

In more recent editions, for instance, 《辭海》(*Ci Hai*) 1961, 1979 and in the Chinese Language Dictionary by Luo (1988), the two characters 創造 (*Chuang Zhao*) have been put together to mean the invention of objects and events that never before existed. The term creativity (創造力) appears in Shu's 1986 edition, meaning the power or strength to make or produce any event or object with new ideas. In Xia's 1999 edition, creativity implies the ability to rework accumulated knowledge and experiences scientifically to produce new concepts, new know-ledge, new thinking. In general, it entails four abilities: to perceive, memorise, think and imagine.

The Chinese definition of creativity as 'the sum of the mental abilities in-volved when people are engaging in creative activities ...' is widely accepted (Wang *et al*, 1998:29). The mental abilities are categorised under intelligence and non-intelligence. The intelligence factor is made up of general abilities (observation, attention, the ability to memorise, operate, and seek attention), logical thinking, and non-logical or creative thinking (imagination, inspiration, intuition, insights, and ability to appreciate). The non-intelligence factor comprises interest, affection, perseverance and quality of character (Wang *et al*, 1998:30). These authors identify three types of creativity: Type A creativity, which brings unprecedented outcomes to humankind and sets the stage for a particular domain of knowledge. Type B creativity also produces novel outcomes but the scope of influence exerted by the outcome does not equal that of type A creativity since the discoveries are within the framework of an existing theory or principle. Type C creativity produces outcomes which are not new to humankind or even the immediate environment, but which are certainly new or a breakthrough for the person doing the creating. This is self-actualising creativity, requiring courage, freedom and risk-taking. Creativity of all three types can be promoted through education and training, as well as the individual's own efforts. Each individual might achieve type C, then type B, and eventually reach type A creativity (Wang *et al*, 1998).

In his book about the characteristics of children's creative ability, Dong Qi offered a relatively consistent definition of creativity: 'the ability to apply the acquired information to produce a novel, unique product or outcome which has social or personal values and for a certain purpose' (1995:2). Novelty means that the outcome does not conform to old rules, but stands out from the old ones and has not existed in the past. Uniqueness refers to something that is unusual and shows deep thought. A product that has social value is something which contributes to the improvement of humankind, the nation and society. The outcome could be in the form of art, literature or science. However, something that has personal value is also meaningful for the development of the individual (Dong, 1995). Creativity involves applying knowledge to new situations and establishing new relationships amongst items of information (Dong, 1995). A creative activity must have clear purpose and not be uselessly fantasised. Dong contrasted creativity with imitation: imitation is a response to the observation of other people's behaviours and activities by manifesting the observed in the same or similar ways. Yet creativity starts with imitation, which Dong considered an important element of the ability to learn.

Li (2000) tried to distinguish the differences between creativity, discovery, invention and innovation and concluded that all have the same connotation: novelty. But each has a special meaning in its own right. To Li, creativity means 'the thinking and behaviour of a brand new inspirational outcome or materialistic outcome of a person' (2000:2). For an outcome to be creative, it must meet the key criterion of being new or acquired for the first time, and so original. Creative outcomes could take different forms but they must be unprecedented and never have existed before. 'Newness is the core feature of creativity' (Li, 2000:3).

Scholar Chunru Hui examined the meanings of creativity in the Chinese language. As a noun, it refers to an ability which empowers someone to produce unique outcomes. As an adjective (creative), it means possessing genuine creativity or possessing something less than genuine creativity. Genuine creativity could produce an outcome that is original to humankind whereas that which is less good might also be unique but is original to its creator only. The verb 'create' means an activity or phenomenon which might lead to the production of certain outcomes, whereas creativity is 'the ability possessed by a person which might produce a unique outcome' (Hui, 1999:1124). Hui acknowledged that creativity is a multi-faceted entity, but he identified it as comprising observation, lateral thinking, flexibility in thinking, the ability to summarise concepts, transfer experiences, associate thoughts, memorise ideas, evaluate situations, and foresee the unknown, which together form an ability structure.

These are some of the interpretations by Chinese scholars of creativity. Some focus on the quality of mental abilities, personality and non-logical thinking in the production of a new outcome, so regard the process as the main concern (eg Wang *et al*, 1998). Others, such as Dong (1995), explained the meaning of creativity in terms of the quality and purpose of a product. Hui (1999) stressed the uniqueness of an outcome as a sign of creativity whereas to Li (2000) creativity is rather about the novelty of an outcome. The definition provided by reference books informs us that creativity involves reworking acquired knowledge before an outcome can be produced.

Several common features can be observed. Importantly, novelty or originality is the key criterion. Also, tangible or intangible outcomes would result from creative activities. Dong, Wang and Hui all state that there are different levels of creativity. The Chinese literature also mentions non-logical thinking (imagination, insights, intuition, etc), the application of accumulated knowledge and skills, and involvement of different mental or cognitive abilities (attention, observation, memorisation, etc).

In sum, it seems that the different theories about creativity stem not only from these Chinese scholars' philosophical positions but also from their interpretations of Western theories on creativity. Nonetheless, their theories emphasise the importance of accumulated knowledge, skills and the presence of cognitive abilities. This is not how creativity is interpreted in the Western literature, where imagination, flexibility, avoiding imitation and being unconventional are identified as the main characteristics.

Interpretations of creativity in the sample cities
Zhuhai SER

The official documents governing kindergarten education in mainland China are concerned mainly with the management, operation and the environmental conditions of kindergartens. Even though the term creativity is mentioned in the documents for promoting children's abilities, none has explicitly explained what the government thinks creativity is. Even in the latest official document, the Guidelines for Kindergarten Education – Trial Version, creativity, although mentioned in association with the domain of the Arts, is not defined. The Guidelines merely emphasises that adults should

> offer opportunities for children to reveal themselves freely, encourage children to express their feelings, understanding and imagination in different forms of arts, respect each child's ideas and creation, accept and assure them of their unique aesthetic sense and forms of manifestation, and share the happiness of creation. (You Er Jiao Yu, 2001: 6)

The instructions suggest that

> the process to create and the outcomes are important means for children to express their knowledge and feelings, [adults] should support children's expressions which carry their personality and creativeness, [adults] should overcome the preference for over-emphasising skills and standardisation. (*You Er Jiao Yu*, 2001:6)

Art is the only one of the five core domains of learning stated in the document which is considered to embrace creativity. Yet in the absence

of a definition, it seems that practitioners have either to rely on literature for understanding what creativity is or interpret this human capacity in light of their own teaching experiences.

Macao SAR

In Macao SAR, the Chief Administrator emphasised in his Annual Policy
Address in 2002 and 2003 that fostering children with creative minds is
important in the new era and should be promoted in foundation education in Macao (Macao Special Administrative Region, Chief Administrator's Annual Policy Address, 2002 and 2003). According to a publication by the Education and Youth Affairs Bureau of Macao SAR, creativity
is an ability which comprises the five elements of divergent thinking:
sensitivity, fluency, flexibility, originality and elaboration. This booklet
is based on work of Taiwanese scholars whose work is in turn derived
from American studies on creativity in the 1960s and 1970s.

The personality traits of creative people have been described as: confident and decisive, childlike, curious, loving to face difficulties, determined, independent, enjoying taking risks and exploring limits,
imaginative, always questioning and believing in intuition, humorous
and having a good memory (*Aomen te bie xing zheng qu jiao yu ji qing
nian ju*, 2002:12). Creative teaching (創思教學) is considered as a pedagogical model that could fulfill the objectives of fostering creativity in
young children. The publication suggests that this pedagogical model
'requires teachers to make use of the contents of the curriculum and
design teaching activities to stimulate and enhance the growth of
students' creative behaviours' (p33). It requires teachers to use 'creative
teaching strategies, together with the curriculum, to allow students to
apply their imagination and foster their thinking ability, which em-
bodies sensitivity, fluency, flexibility, originality, and elaboration' (p33).
The creative teaching strategies recommended can be summarised
thus:

- ask – apply questioning techniques during discussions and
  provide guidance for thinking

- think – give children time to think about those questions

- practise – put ideas into the production of outcomes

- evaluate – give children opportunities to reflect on their ideas and the quality of their work.

The publication states that this pedagogical model does not conflict with traditional teaching and learning but that the two are complementary. But it offers no review of the different perspectives and definitions of creativity, possibly giving readers the impression that the meaning of creativity is straightforward. Whether or not the Education and Youth Bureau in Macao SAR is aware that there are disparities in the interpretation of creativity in both the West and mainland China is unclear – what they have is a set of Western ideas of creativity that they want to promote.

Practitioners, scholars and their government often hold different views of an educational idea. The discrepancies can form barriers to actualising ideas and putting them into practice. Facing pressure for reform, researchers and practitioners in China advocate several practical pedagogical strategies in response to the call for creative education.

Chinese pedagogical strategies for fostering creativity

Those interested in creativity and early years learning have discussed the conditions that favour fostering creativity in young children. After reviewing both Western and Chinese studies, Yuan (2000) outlined six conditions and approaches needed to promote children's development in creativity. They are: providing a safe and supportive learning environment, emphasising the process instead of the outcomes of learning activities, discouraging children from imitating others' work, giving children options, providing guidance and assistance to facilitate learning and alleviate frustrations and, finally, modifying the physical environment from time to time and designing open-ended activities for children. Liu (1997) emphasised that conditions which extend children's ideas, stimulate their imagination and lift constraints on expression of ideas will facilitate their creative development.

Liu (1997) described how classroom activities can be play-oriented and promote creativity. Collecting artwork materials, studying them and thinking about, choosing from, and making something out of these materials will draw children's attention to the nature, properties and relationship between them. If they explore the possibilities in the making process, children are more likely to apply their creative thinking in a free, stimulating, encouraging, supportive, accepting environment in which they can work on tasks independently and confidently. However, Liu, like others, does not explain what he means by creativity – he simply defines it by activities in which participation would somehow produce a particular understanding of it. Liu maintains that basic skills are necessary for creativity and imagination to take off. Teachers' guidance and demonstrations at the initial stage of an activity are required and if given an opportunity, the children will try their best to create afterwards.

Not all Chinese early childhood educators agree on whether it is necessary to demonstrate to children the way to do things. Jin (2001) proposed that in order to foster children's creativity through arts (music, dancing, drawing and painting, etc) direct demonstrations for the children should be avoided. Demonstrations provide children with opportunities to copy adults' work but will jeopardise creative thinking. However, Ji (2003) took the stance that imitation precedes creation and normally people enter the mode of creativity through the process of observing and imitating other people's work. This fits with the Vygotskian stance of learning, which depends on the learner being a close observer who imitates the teacher's moves. So how do Chinese teachers apply imitation to the classroom to facilitate children's learning?

The approaches employed to foster creativity in young Chinese children include arts education (Song, 2001; Fan, 2001), construction games (Zhang, 2000), physical education (Guo, 2001) and science education (Wang, 2002). Some Chinese educators' approaches to fostering creativity in children through drawing, music and physical education lessons are described below.

Drawing lesson
Fan (2001) suggested that in art education, creativity means different forms of representation, which should be novel, unique, and an expression of one's feelings. The practitioner illustrates that instead of simply requesting children to draw something different from the teacher's drawing – which can supposedly encourage unique ideas – children should be encouraged to express their ideas and feelings about a drawing and even talk about different drawing methods before they attempt

their own drawing (Fan, 2001). Fan believes that children's indepen-dence and autonomy can be fostered in the process of drawing, as teachers can encourage them to select the materials they need and decide on the style of drawing, thus allowing them to actualise their own ideas and finish the task independently.

Music lesson

Song (2001) examines the ways by which autonomic musical activities promote creativity. The operational definition of creativity is an ability to use acquired knowledge and experiences to facilitate automatic manipulation and imagination so as to arouse self-initiated explora-tion, imagination and lateral exchanges of ideas toward a particular goal. Song believes that autonomic musical activities can stimulate children to explore and freely manipulate the different musical tunes with both traditional (piano, accordion, violin, etc) and non-traditional (bottles, cans, etc) musical instruments provided by adults. Imagina-tion could be activated through body language as this is one of the most natural ways to express one's feelings. Most children will apply their ex-periences to create body movements that inform the audience about the kind of music they are hearing. A learning environment which faci-litates children's social interactions with teachers and peers will en-courage them not only to express their thoughts and actions but also to exchange their ideas, and this might develop their creativity.

Physical education lesson

If the teaching objectives are designed to nurture creativity, physical education activities would also have something to offer. Guo (2000) says that teachers must themselves be creative so they can influence the children, verbally and physically. The learning atmosphere must be democratic, and discussions between teachers and children are wel-come. Components of a game can be integrated into physical educa-tion. Game-like activities are helpful in encouraging eagerness in think-ing, active exploration and promoting imagination, confidence, sense of achievement, and ability to innovate. Explanations of an activity should be modified into a discussion of the possible ways of doing the exercise, leaving time and space for children to explore their ideas and imagine the possibilities. In informal physical education lessons, adults should encourage children to use the objects or equipment flexibly and imaginatively so as to stretch their interest and creativity.

In short, Chinese teachers' efforts to promote creativity in children vary across disciplines. However, the authors have not explained what is so creative about these activities. They have not illustrated explicitly how they read these activities as being creative so provide only assumptions. More succinct evidence would be helpful in understanding what Chinese kindergarten teachers mean by creativity and how they go about fostering it.

Where do the theories on cognitive development stand?

It appears that the Piagetian theory of learning has had the deepest influence on Chinese theorising about early years learning as it was imported several decades ago. Adults were urged to pay attention to the learning environment and ensure children's active role in learning. But not all Western ideas have been accepted. For example, most Chinese scholars accept that children should take part actively in learning activities but they reject the pure form of child-centred approach which sees the child as the main figure in learning who constructs knowledge through interactions with the environment without much guidance from the teachers. This view might reflect a culture-specific perspective of the teachers' role in children's learning, but because the child-centred approach relies upon a teacher facilitating the learning opportunities, it is not entirely independent of teachers.

It is more an issue of the forms this guidance takes. This is evident in the pedagogical strategies to foster creativity which still focus on the impact of teachers' guidance on children's learning, especially their role in lesson planning, direct teaching of skills, and demonstration of the correct way to do things. It seems that the mastery of skills acquired through imitation is important in fostering creativity and forms a key theme running through the Chinese definitions and theories about creativity, the view of learning and the pedagogical strategies. Taken together, it appears that by scrutinising the definitions and theories of creativity, the line distinguishing the Piagetian from the Vygotskian ideas of cognition and learning begins to blur. This possibility certainly warrants further research and exploration.

Furthermore, even though the pedagogical strategies for promoting Chinese children's creativity, as described in the literature, urge the provision of conditions that allow for open-ended activities, a more democratic learning atmosphere and a relatively control-free environment, whether these conditions can be put into practice very much depends on the early childhood educators in the schools. Whether demonstrations or direct teaching are necessary when fostering creativity is still debatable. It seems that teachers are attempting to stretch the limits of the subject areas that are of value to the kindergarten education in their own ways and according to their understanding of what it is to be creative.

The literature about issues of creativity in early childhood education which I have reviewed provides a framework for the study of the educational reforms undertaken in the cities in my study. The education departments in both mainland China and Macao SAR have attempted to explain the importance of fostering creativity in young children, what creativity means, directly and indirectly, and how it should be fostered. Given the different historical backgrounds of the cities, and the varied interpretations of creativity and the pedagogical strategies, we can expect similarities and differences in what is observed where the fostering of creativity is evolving.

We turn now to the two sites of this study and learn from them the school cultures that have permeated the classrooms and school ethos.

4

A kindergarten in a city with two cultures

The One Country, Two Systems Policy was enforced in 1999 when Macao was handed over to the Chinese Government. However, Macao SAR is safeguarded by the Basic Laws which entitle it to high autonomy for 50 years in its jurisdiction system, religious beliefs, social and education system. In reality, since the hand-over, any changes in Macao SAR have been slow and subtle.

Macao SAR: Background to kindergarten education

Most of the kindergartens in Macao SAR are private institutions, owned by religious groups, local organisations, and foundations. Only a small number of public kindergartens are owned by the government. At the time the data for this study was collected, there were six public and about 55 private kindergartens. The public kindergartens are easily distinguished by their names as they are either in Portuguese or labelled *Luso-Chinês*. The *Luso-Chinês* kindergartens are Chinese speaking, but offer Portuguese instead of English on the curriculum, even though the emphasis diminished after 1999. Both private and public kindergartens provide services for children from 3 to 6 years old. During this study, I found that the private kindergartens in Macao SAR focused on facilitating the cognitive development of their pupils. They prioritise mathematics, Chinese language and writing, and English and marginalise arts and sports.

Even before the Portuguese era in Macao SAR ended in 1999, some effort was made by the local education authority to improve the school curricula and the Curriculum Reform Group of the Education and Youth Affairs Bureau of Macao SAR has played a leading role. Initially, the members of the team were contracted from Portugal, Hong Kong and Macao and the first edition of the curriculum was completed in 1999. However, the curriculum guidelines designed and revised by the Curriculum Reform Group have only been implemented in government owned schools and kindergartens, so private kindergartens, for historical reasons, remain independent of local education authority monitoring. These *Luso-Chinês* kindergartens are characterised by their Portuguese style which is quite different from the private kindergartens owned by local organisations, religious groups or individuals. The *Luso-Chinês* kindergartens differ substantially from the privately-owned ones in terms of resources, teacher-child ratio, philosophy, as well as curriculum. There is no easy answer to whether they are better or worse than private kindergartens. To make things more complicated, the privately-owned schools have different curricula and the programmes are driven by different philosophies so some are still very traditional while others are eager to change. The traditional ones follow conventional ways of teaching, and focus on writing and reading. The innovative kindergartens have adopted some Western pedagogical ideas about early childhood education. Clearly, these variations raise questions about the quality of the curricula.

The reasons for the marked differences between the private kindergartens go back to the previous Portuguese government, which made no effort to establish the education system in Macao. So the private schools including kindergartens had much freedom, and resources and development were concentrated on public kindergartens. By and large, the Education and Youth Affairs Bureau barely exercised its authority to intervene in the local private schools, but lately intervention has increased through measures such as the school assessment scheme and the implementation of fee-free foundation education.

According to Wong (1999), the *laissez-faire* policy described above had pros and cons. The private kindergartens had plenty of freedom to outline their own philosophy and ideology, manage their financial accounts, set up the curriculum model and choose teaching materials.

But they lacked financial support from the Government and resources were sparse. Before the previous Portuguese Government offered assistance to the local Chinese schools and kindergartens, European missionaries in Macao established schools and educated the local children at almost no cost. Even though the missionaries might thus spread their doctrines, their contribution to education in Macao will always be remembered. Since the 1970s, various government decisions were made to meet the expectations of local educators. For instance, after the 1977 decree, private kindergartens received some subsidies and were exempted from taxation (Liu, 1999). In 1995, a 29/95/M law was enforced which declared that the 10 years of 'fee-free education policy' should cover the last year of kindergarten education, the six years of primary education, and the first three years of secondary education (Wong, 1999).

Developing under the influence of two mainstream cultures gives Macao SAR a special charisma. The colonial period brought with it ordeals and a special status for the Chinese in Macao SAR. Social and educational changes were dramatic. But they now face new challenges, including those arising from yet another educational reform.

The need for creativity in Macao SAR

The need for reform built up gradually. The colonial government had paid little attention to education for the Chinese, and the private schools developed their own curriculum and philosophy before the mid 80s. Recently, the Macao SAR government realised that a new local curriculum was needed, including new teaching materials for the traditional kindergartens. It sought to change the focus of learning from word recognition, rote learning and practising Chinese characters, to a balanced curriculum featuring Arts, Music and Physical Education, Morality, Chinese, Mathematics and Environmental Education. This will be a long process. The importance of teaching for creative thinking was first announced by the Macao SAR Chief Administrator's Annual Policy Addresses in 2002 and 2003 and signified the essential qualities of creative teaching and learning. Two public kindergartens took responsibility to experiment with a new pedagogical model. One of these was Girassol Kindergarten.

Understanding the school culture of Girassol Kindergarten

As a public kindergarten under the Education and Youth Affairs Bureau Girassol Kindergarten began the Creative Teaching model in two K3 classes (5 to 6 year-olds). The new teaching strategy is based on the understanding of the Bureau's theories of creativity and the Project Approach described in Chapter 2. Art work activities used junk materials as exemplified by the Project Approach to promote children's creativity. I was privileged to witness the experimental period of this new pedagogy. I use the multi-layering method of Gregory and Williams (2000) to analyse the nature of the kindergarten culture I observed.

The historical background and stated philosophy of any kindergarten are vital to its existence so these are presented as an outer layer. The middle layer comprises an examination of how the outer layer affects how the classes, curriculum, care-taking policies and pedagogical approaches are organised – the daily routine, home-school relationships, lessons and classroom settings. These two layers create the inner layer – the school culture. Only when this culture is fairly clear can we understand the relationship between it and the individuals functioning in it. Chart A illustrates the intricacy of these different layers.

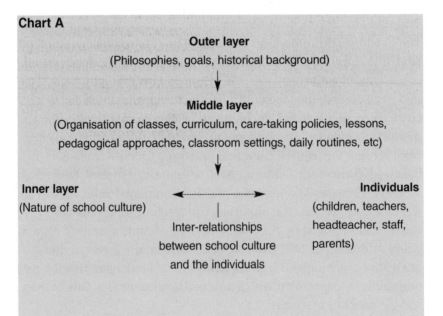

Chart A

Outer layer
(Philosophies, goals, historical background)

Middle layer
(Organisation of classes, curriculum, care-taking policies, lessons, pedagogical approaches, classroom settings, daily routines, etc)

Inner layer   **Individuals**
(Nature of school culture)   (children, teachers,
                                                                                        headteacher, staff,
Inter-relationships   parents)
between school culture
and the individuals

Outer layer – the social context

The social context of Girassol Kindergarten is discussed in terms of its historical background and philosophy. According to the headteacher, the mission of government-owned kindergartens was and still is to provide children from poor families and new immigrants from mainland China with affordable early childhood education.

Since the Chinese government adopted the Open Door Policy, many mainland Chinese who had relatives in Macao moved there in the 1980s for family reunions, job opportunities and a better standard of living. Most of these immigrants were of low social and economic status. Likewise, many Filipino immigrants of similar status came to Macao looking for job opportunities and a better standard of living.

The removal of the kindergarten to the new site was tied to social and demographic changes during the colonial time.

> Researcher: *What was the reason for the move?*

> Headteacher Leong: *... as the birthrate went down, together with various other reasons, a lot of new immigrants might, they might have arrived at Macao for a certain period of time. They might have transferred to the central or other districts [for work]. As far as living is concerned, they would move to this district. In 1997, we moved here. This was a brand new district, only a small number of schools in the neighbourhood, two to three kindergartens ... after moving to this district, this new Girassol, in terms of student numbers, was quite full.* (Girassol, 19 Nov. 2002)

At the time, Girassol had been at its current site for five years. There were 6 classes (two classes for 3-year-olds, two for 4-year-olds, and two pre-primary preparatory classes for 5-year-olds) and the total number of children was about 150.

At the time of the interview, the headteacher had been in her post for four years. She explained that the philosophy of the kindergarten has been stated in an official document called the Macao Education System (澳門教育制度) under the law 11/91/M.

> Headteacher Leong: *Eh ... in fact, there is ... eh ... a Macao Education System. We follow this system. In it, it is mentioned that early childhood*

education is called pre-school, and there is also pre-primary preparatory education. As for the ideology, it hopes to foster students to ... eh ... have ... eh ... foster students to be able to adapt to the new learning environment, and this, when the teachers are designing [the activities and learning contents], will do it according to the needs of the children, ... eh ... their individual needs. Eh ... it also fosters pupils' mental and physical health, eh ... the various, the five educational goals (include) moral, intellectual, physical, social, aesthetical development. (Girassol, 19 Nov. 2002)

The headteacher was referring to the goals stated in the Macao Education System for early childhood education, which she personally agreed to. But she explained that even though they have to observe the goals stated in the official document, each government-owned kindergarten is given space for school development. As Girassol has a large number of children from immigrant families, their emphasis is on establishing positive home-school relationships.

Middle layer – Organisation of programme and curriculum

Since the Chinese Government regained sovereignty over Macao SAR in 1999, Girassol has always flown the Chinese National flag. The Portuguese scripts of the school name on the main building contrast interestingly with the Chinese National flag and their co-existence reminds people of the historical changes the kindergarten has gone through.

The government-owned kindergartens in Macao SAR have adapted to the post-colonial era with their historical mission to continue serving the disadvantaged in Macao and also to keep Portuguese as a subject. Their programmes, charges, and enrolment requirements have there-

Photo 2: The main building of Girassol Kindergarten with the Chinese National flag hoisted at the front gate

fore remained unchanged. However, as the new administrative government sets direction for the education arena, the curriculum and pedagogy of government-owned schools like Girassol Kindergarten needs to be modified. I collected the data on the organisation and curriculum of the kindergarten during field visits via documentary evidence, fieldnotes, visual data and my daily journal.

Routines and provision of care

Since most children at Girassol are from poor families, food and care are provided at the kindergarten. A timetable for 5-year-old children in the 2001/2002 academic year, before it embarked on the Project Approach, is presented in Table A on page 46. Breakfast, lunch, snacks, outdoor playtime and nap time are guaranteed.

Communication with parents

The headteacher emphasised the importance placed on home-school cooperation. Hence, for each academic year, Girassol Kindergarten at very low cost organises different activities such as seminars, picnics, children's artwork exhibitions, road safety day and gardening day, etc. Since the parents work long hours, the hope is that they can take part in at least one of these activities during the year. A bulletin board in the lobby gives parents information about the activities in the local district such as Chinese opera shows, free pottery classes, the new schedule of the local library and other notices.

As well as encouraging parents to take part in these on and off-campus activities, personal contacts with parents are valued. Parents' meetings are held on weekends or evenings so as to fit the schedule of most parents. In certain cases, meetings are held over the telephone or teachers have to pay home visits.

Supervisions, formal lessons and extended activities

From the time the children arrive, they are closely supervised by teachers. From morning exercises, toilet time, meal time, submission of homework, to group (table) activities in the afternoon, children follow precise rules and instructions. The photos illustrate some of the rules and regulations.

Traditionally in Chinese schools, subject matter considered important for children to learn is scheduled in the morning when children are

Hours	Monday	Tuesday	Wednesday	Thursday	Friday
9:00-9:20A.M.	Arrival/Outdoor	↑	↑	↑	↑
9:20-9:40	Breakfast	↑	↑	↑	↑
9:40-10:10	Thematic lesson	↑	↑	↑	↑
10:10-10:30	Computer activities	Practise Chinese writing	Computer activities	Creative games	Computer activities
10:30-11:00	Playground	↑	↑	↑	↑
11:00-12:15	Portuguese lesson	↑	↑	↑	↑
12:15-1:00P.M.	Lunch	↑	↑	↑	↑
1:00-2:25	Nap time	↑	↑	↑	↑
2:25-2:30	Clean up	↑	↑	↑	↑
2:30-2:50	Playground	↑	↑	↑	↑
2:50-3:20	Music (combine K3s)	↑	↑	↑	↑
3:20-4:20	Snack & group (table) activities	Snack & creative games	Snack & group (table) activities	Snack & group (table) activities	Snack & group (table) activities
4:20-4:30	Tidy up	↑	↑	↑	↑

Table A: Timetable for K3 classes of Girassol Kindergarten

Photo 3: Picture cards of the proper way to wash hands were posted in the toilet.

Photo 4: Cartoon children serve as role models for proper way to walk up the stairs

energetic and focused after a night's sleep, and the less important activities are fitted into the afternoon schedule. At Girassol, time and space are arranged according to this viewpoint. The 5-year-old children at Girassol have one session of Portuguese each morning but the Chinese lesson, also known as thematic lesson, was the main course of the school menu. This formal lesson time is teacher-led and children are supposed to answer the teacher's questions in due course.

Extended activities: Teachers at Girassol employ various techniques to help children in their writing. The learning of Chinese characters is mainly through careful observation of each stroke, copying the form of the characters, and then practicing repeatedly.

Photo 5: Teacher's exemplary writing which shows a step by step approach

Photo 6: A poster of the Chinese radicals is posted in the classroom to assist children's learning

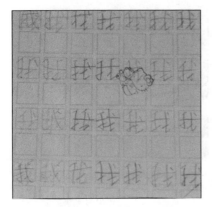

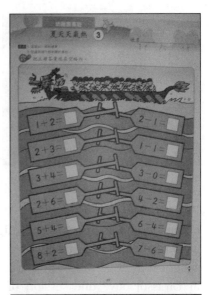

Above: Photo 7: Teacher corrects children's Chinese writing homework by over-writing the characters in red ink
Right: Photo 8: Worksheet on addition and subtraction

Worksheets such as those on solving mathematical problems are also important elements in the children's learning.

Even though Chinese writing and mathematical concepts are rated important in children's learning, the teachers try to make sure that there is a balance to each day by including, for example, drawing and handicraft in the extended activity time. The following photos (10-12) present some of the artwork produced by children before the pedagogical approach changed. It is about the theme 'People who help us – Policemen'. These products are all remarkably similar in the ideas and materials used.

Photo 9: Worksheet on consecutive numbers

Photo 10: Binoculars police officers use

Photo 11: Watches police officers use

Photo 12: Walkie-talkies police officers use

The two K3 classrooms are divided into different centres: art, science, toy (puzzles, games), reading, family, and an area for tables and chairs. The reading centre is carpeted and is also used for lesson time or carpet time but it can only be visited when writing and mathematics assignments are finished.

Photo 13: From left to right: toy centre, art centre and science centre

Photo 14: Reading centre is situated under the window

Below. Photo 15: Family centre is across from the reading centre

A special feature of the classroom is the trail of footprints on the floor. The footprints go around the tables in one direction. When children need to move around the classroom, for example, to get lunch or submit homework, they have to follow the trail. It is intended to control traffic in the classroom.

Most of the teaching resources are either prepared by the teachers or commercially produced. Girassol teachers also rely on workbooks and grid exercise books to reinforce conceptual development and learning. The materials for artwork are primarily commercial products such as different kinds of coloured paper, cotton balls, paint, crayon, etc. plus paper roll centres and milk cartons. Children are allowed to use the materials as they choose, whatever their source.

Inner layer – the school culture of Girassol Kindergarten
A few special features of Girassol Kindergarten give it its unique culture.

- Although the children are from disadvantaged families, the resources, materials, staff and food in this kindergarten are both quality and quantity assured.

- There is little artificial or grand decoration. On display in the classrooms and corridors is mostly the children's work. More importantly, teachers are friendly and willing to share with parents the life of their children at school and various opportunities were given for parents to talk personally with teachers. The team contrives to narrow the gap between home and school in numerous ways.

- As the timetable shows, Girassol Kindergarten has contrived to provide children with a balanced curriculum during lesson time and in extended activities. It respects different aspects of children's development but the focus remains on the acquisition of mathematical concepts, general knowledge and writing skill.

- Girassol offers language lessons in Portuguese to K3 children and involves the native-speaking Portuguese teacher in bringing other elements to the school. As well as taking care of the Portuguese lessons, she is understood to be responsible for fostering children's imagination and creativity. The headteacher and class teachers agree that the Portuguese teacher is very creative. Her artwork and that produced by pupils are often displayed in the main entrance. Vong *sin san* (*sin san* means teacher in Cantonese), one of the class teachers in this study, once said to me:

Alicia (name of the Portuguese teacher) is very creative. The Portuguese teachers are really different. If you ask me to make those artworks, I just can't. But she does it so easily and quickly. (Journal: Girassol, 28 February, 2002)

■ Although the school curriculum is reasonably balanced, the children's activities are structured into meal times, lesson times, and extended (group) activity time. Priority was given to children's intellectual development: the acquisition of literacy and mathematical concepts.

This is a warm kindergarten with well organised teachers who had structured children's activities and conducted lessons in a teacher-led style before their pedagogy changed.

School culture and the individual – the inter-relationships
School and children
Despite the low social economic status of their families, most children were quite self confident. Many were confident and eloquent during class discussions. They would show me their handicrafts and sometimes told me what their drawings were about. They were very observant and detail oriented due to the importance placed on Chinese writing and mathematics which demand concentration and attention to detail. However, their artwork shows little independent thinking in their use of materials and ideas. Most children would comply with the teachers' instructions and rules and imitate what others had done, resulting in similar products. The children were friendly to their classmates including the Filipinos.

School and teacher
The head and other teachers made up a caring and conscientious team. As the teachers always had to supervise the children closely during routines, lesson time and even activity time, the tone and words they used were rather authoritarian. But they cared deeply about the chil-

dren's performance at school and their attitude toward learning. On a few occasions, they shared these concerns with me. Most of the teachers, including the head, had upgraded their qualifications through in-service training and they attended seminars and conferences organised by the Education and Youth Affairs Bureau or the city's teacher training institute so as to update their knowledge about early childhood education and related issues such as parent and home co-operation schemes. Whether the incentive for participating in these activities was out of genuine interest or due to pressure from the Education and Youth Affairs Bureau, the fact is that the teachers updated their professional knowledge in early childhood education from time to time.

School and parents
The parents' participation in classroom activities and meetings were not observed in this study, but the headteacher claimed that the participation rate was usually satisfactory. The teachers would advise the parents of new pupils about issues such as how to apply for social welfare, and how to communicate with their children effectively. But according to the teachers, despite their efforts at strengthening their relationship with the parents, some parents were reluctant to take part in the special events and activities or even talk to them. They could only look at the positive feedback and concentrate on their jobs.

5

Kindergartens in a city with a single culture

This chapter examines a public kindergarten in Zhuhai SER, Customs Kindergarten. It too is changing its pedagogical approaches under the current education reform in mainland China. Zhuhai SER is part of mainland China so is geographically, politically and socially under one system. This signifies that, even though Zhuhai is a special economic region, most of its Chinese teachers share more similarities with those in other parts of China than those in Macao SAR.

Zhuhai SER: Background of kindergarten education

There are both private kindergartens (owned by private individuals, organisations in the business sector, joint-partnership of foreign and local investments) and public (owned by the government departments such as the Women's Association, The Customs and The Revenue Bureau) in Zhuhai SER. The private kindergartens provide a service for all children in the city but the public ones give priority to children whose parents work in its departments or offices. Most kindergartens are open long hours (7:30am to 6:00pm) for children aged 3 to 6. Others provide boarding services and children go home only once a week. As well as education, this service includes providing breakfast, lunch, nap-time, snacks and after school interest groups where children can learn dancing, drawing, Chinese chess, playing musical instruments. The idea is that with the children in good hands, their parents can concentrate on their careers. At the time of the study, there were about 200 kindergartens, serving 32,000 children. Only six were public.

At the time of data collection, the operation and management of kindergarten education in Zhuhai SER were under the supervision of two local authorities, the Zhuhai City Education Committee – Kindergarten Section (established in 1990), and the *Xienzhou* Region Education Committee (*Xienzhou* is a district in Zhuhai SER). These authorities oversee the kindergartens registered at their offices. All kindergartens in China have to observe two official documents issued by the National Education Commission. One is the Kindergarten Management Regulations (幼兒園管理條例), issued in August 1989, which outlines the requirements for setting up a kindergarten, the relevant legal issues, and the administrative role of the Government. The other is the Statute for Kindergartens (幼兒園工作規程) which outlines the nature and goals of kindergarten education, guidelines for enrolment procedures, operating conditions of a kindergarten, suggestions for the physical environment and facilities, guidelines for parental education, and the managerial structure of a kindergarten. Under the guidance of the Zhuhai City Education Committee, kindergartens in the county, town, and city have been supervised since 1990 according to their category. The ranking system for kindergartens belonging to the different categories was first introduced in the same year. The performance index of the ranking system has been developed by the joint efforts of officials from the Zhuhai City Education Committee – Kindergarten Section, and a group of headteachers, mostly from the public kindergartens.

As with Macao, the private kindergartens enjoy greater autonomy than the public kindergartens in terms of curriculum design, philosophy, finance, and staff management. From 1979 to 1990, kindergartens mainly followed a standard set of teaching objectives and materials. Since 1990, different curriculum models have been put into practice by different private kindergartens, such as the Thematic Approach and the Montessori Approach. The Project Approach and the Reggio Emilia curriculum have created a forum for discussions. Even after 1990, the public kindergartens strictly follow the National Curriculum Guidelines, and other kindergarten educational models could be put on a trial basis. Each private kindergarten has its own philosophy and sets up its own teaching goals, but most would choose to fulfill those outlined in the National Teaching Objective Guideline on which the ranking system

56

is based. While private kindergartens receive no financial support from the Chinese Government but are exempted from taxation, financial support and other subsidies are granted to public kindergartens by local government so the tuition rate at these kindergartens remains low, to benefit government officials.

The Central, Municipal and educational entities

Every kindergarten in Zhuhai SER has to observe the policies, documents, and regulations issued at the National, Provincial, and Municipal level. The local educational authorities are responsible for planning and organising activities (with reference to the policies, documents, and regulations) for local kindergartens. These activities might include regular meetings, visits to other kindergartens, different contests and competitions for teachers and children, and appraisals for the kindergartens. These plans are made known to all kindergartens at the beginning of the year by the supervising authority. Likewise, the guidelines for reforming the educational system, such as the National Education Affairs '95' Plan (國家教育事務 '九五' 計劃), is passed on to each kindergarten at locally organised meetings or through distribution of relevant documents. These plans are designed at national level every five years. The National Education Affairs '95' Plan is in fact the ninth 5-year-plan designed by the National Education Commission in 1995 and the tenth was announced in 2001.

The number of kindergartens in Zhuhai SER increased as its economic status improved and the population expanded. The ownership of the kindergartens varies but this is endorsed by Central Government. Even though the kindergartens have to observe the policies and regulations designed by Central Government, there is still some leeway for provision, especially for private kindergartens. However, as the Guidelines for Early Childhood Education – Trial Version is being implemented in mainland Chinese cities, kindergartens in Zhuhai SER have to abide by the same document. Consequently fostering creativity in young children has become one of the goals of kindergartens in Zhuhai SER.

The school culture of Customs Kindergarten

Like Girassol, Customs Kindergarten has adopted some ideas from the Project Approach, especially in art work activities, while maintaining the Chinese language as the focus of their curriculum. This modification of the curriculum and pedagogy serve as a response to the expectation of fostering creativity in children. The multi-layering method of Gregory and Williams (2000) is again used to analyse the kindergarten culture. The similarities and differences observed in the Girassol and Customs cultures do not mean that one is superior to the other. The information collected through interviews, photos, documentary evidence, fieldnotes, and my journals will be analysed in order to learn about the Customs kindergarten.

An outer layer – the social context

Again, my main source of information is the headteacher. The historical and philosophical issues of Customs Kindergarten were discussed during the interview.

Customs Kindergarten was established in 1957 under the Customs Department of the Zhuhai government, until when entire Customs Department occupied a large courtyard. The original two low bungalows were demolished and replaced by the current building in 1990. When it began the service it provided was informal: the so-called child care service entailed no more than looking after the children's health and safety; there were not many children; and instead of qualified teachers, some old ladies were hired as temporary workers. As well as rebuilding the kindergarten, the service was formalised by changes in staffing policy.

Funding comes from the Customs Department and the children enrolled are mostly the offspring of the officers. Non-officer families pay three times more as priority is given to children whose parents are government officials in all the government-owned kindergartens in Zhuhai SER. Hence, most children at the Customs Kindergarten are from families with fairly high social and economic status.

At the time of the interview, Customs Kindergarten had been at its present site for eleven years, housing a total of about 350 children aged from 2 to 6 years old. There were eleven classes altogether – one nursery class, three classes for 4-year-olds, three for 5-year-olds, three for 5 to 6-year-olds and one pre-primary class.

Customs Kindergarten has quite a long history, so its philosophy and goals have changed over the years, along with the expansion of the Customs Department, social changes, and the educational ideas of the various headteachers. But there has always been a focus on children's mental and physical health. This might be because the government officers have to comply strictly with the One-child Policy. The head-teacher said that the official document, Statute for Kindergartens, has guided their curriculum. So the philosophy and goals of Customs Kindergarten are formed by the headteacher's educational ideas, understanding of the government's expectations, and the wish to accommodate social change. Under headteacher Chen's management, Customs Kindergarten strives to achieve many goals.

The headteacher also emphasised the significance of creative education in the educational arena of mainland China. She has not only heard of creative education, but also appreciated the idea.

> Headteacher Chen: *In 1998, the third national conference on educa-tion was held. At that time, Jiang Zhe Min [Chair of the PRC from 1996-2003] mentioned that to nurture the Chinese ethnicity, actualise quality education, improve the quality of the entire ethnicity, at that time crea-tive education was mentioned as the core of quality education. ... Then the education committee published a series of requirements about crea-tive education, I have read them seriously. I thought that it was a marvellous suggestion...*

She told me that certain political and theoretical frameworks underpin her education ideology, along with her own reflections on the Chinese education system. She is fully supportive of creative education and of fostering creative thinking in children.

Middle layer – organisation of programmes and curriculum

The breadth of its philosophy and goal of Customs Kindergarten are im-pressive. And it seems that Customs Kindergarten has the conditions to build the children's physical fitness.

Physical conditions for fostering children's fitness

The main building is located within the Customs courtyard. The Chinese national flag is not flown but mounted at the entrance are two cartoon pandas, a precious animal of China, and they give the building

Photo 16: The main building of Customs Kindergarten.

a Chinese flavour. The large windows allow air and light, two important elements for good health, to enter the classrooms and other activity areas. The whole building is raised above the ground so as to create more playground space for physical activities. The Chinese slogan on the building highlights the expectation of teachers at Customs Kindergarten: love children, learn hard, be good at teaching and glad to contribute. The large basket ball field in front of the main building is one of the facilities for the officers which the kindergarten uses for group morning exercises and other outdoor activities. They make some of the outdoor equipment themselves. All these facilities and efforts enable large muscle development and gymnastic skills training.

Routines and care-taking policies
At Customs, teachers and caretakers take great care of the children's health by encouraging them to drink plenty of water, maintaining air ventilation in the classroom and keeping children dry after playground time. The kindergarten also makes sure that children consume a certain amount of food at each meal. The nutritional level of food served is measured by the school nurse. Table 2 shows the timetable of the two classes for 5-year-olds at the time of the field visits. It shows that breakfast, lunch (including fruit), and afternoon snacks are provided and that nap time and playground time are guaranteed.

Photo 17: Children are doing morning exercise in one spring morning

Table 2: Timetable for 5-year-olds at Customs Kindergarten

Time	Activities
7:30 – 8:00 am	Greetings, free playground time
8:00 – 8:40	Breakfast
8:40 – 9:20	Centre activities
9:20 – 10:20	In-between-lesson, morning exercise, physical education and free playground time
10:30 – 11:05	Educational activities
11:05 – 11:15	Preparations for lunch
11:15 – 12:00	Lunch, taking a walk in the campus
12:00 – 2:15 pm	Nap time
2:15 – 2:50	Out of bed, toilet time, snacks
2:50 – 4:00	Games or Centre activities
4:00 – 4:30	Physical education and free playground time
4:30 – 5:00	Physical education and free playground time
5:00 – 5:30	Clean up and pick up time

Communication with parents

Customs Kindergarten belongs to the Customs Department and its mission is to provide education and care services for the officers' children. The relationship between the staff and the parents is complex: while the teachers are respected for what they do for the children, the parents can comment quite freely. So good communication with the parents is essential.

Display boards are used to enhance communication. Any announcements or reminders of important days are posted on a bulletin board and wheeled to the main entrance. The weekly menu is set in the playground area to inform parents of food their children have had at school. A display board near the nurse's office is designated for advice on health issues and prevention of childhood illnesses.

A notice board entitled Window for Home and Kindergarten is mounted outside each classroom. This board carries different messages such as:

- teaching objectives for the week

- teachers' personal feelings about educating the children

- journal articles about early childhood education

- brief descriptions of the children's good deeds or desirable learning attitudes at school

- photographs which introduce special events or show children's experiences

- names of the children scheduled to assist the teachers

The teachers use another green board to state the kinds of help they need from parents (eg supply junk materials to the class, provide information on certain topics, observe certain natural phenomena with children at home) in order to facilitate the project work undertaken in class.

Other means of communication include personal conversations between parents and teachers about the children's personalities, learning attitudes, school performance, etc. The kindergarten also organises all kinds of activities in which parents can participate (eg Little Musicians' Day, Sports' Day, Mid-Autumn or Full Moon Festival Celebration). The headteacher says that, the special events are carefully scheduled and

Photo 18: One of the Window for Home and Kindergarten boards outside each classroom

most parents are eager to join the events and witness the development of their children.

Supervisions, formal lessons and informal activities
Supervisions: In most cases, the children are not strictly disciplined. Supervision takes various forms. Music is used in the classroom all the time to signify desirable behaviours such as cleaning up and returning to seats. Other desirable behaviours are encouraged by learning from role models in photographs.

Whistles are used to signify when it is time for the children to gather together (eg line up before taking the stairs) but most of the time, children are supervised according to their own pace (eg a child can get fruit as soon as she finishes her meal).

Formal lessons: At Customs, the core lessons and activities take place in the morning. During Chinese or thematic lesson time, the class is divided into two groups, with one teacher in charge of each group. The

Photo 19: Laminated photograph which demonstrates the proper way to go down stairs

teachers teach different subjects – one might teach mathematical concepts and the other discuss the current project – exchanging groups the next day. The timetable shown does not reflect all the activities taught and learned in the classroom. I use the term in-between-learning activities to describe the short lessons, usually of ten to fifteen minutes. The in-between-learning activities provide opportunities for learning Chinese pinyin and word recognition, which requires a good deal of practice.

Photo 20: Photographs which demonstrate the required behaviours, procedures and manners at meal times

Photo 21: Book for reading and word recognition

The pedagogical approach adopted by the two teachers is essentially teacher-centred. The teachers give a lecture on the pre-designed contents and the class sits and listens. This lasts the whole lesson. Occasionally, teachers might ask questions about the topic and the children's responses are only for that class discussion. Little of their contribution is used to extend the classroom activities and learning materials, as the teachers have already prepared all the lesson plans for the project, which usually lasts for two weeks. From revisions of Chinese pinyin, thematic lesson, to the teaching of mathematical concepts, teachers' demonstration and lectures are heavily relied upon.

Extended activities: The teachers also use printed matter as aids for teaching and learning, as shown in the following photographs.

These books, exercise books and worksheets are usually used in the afternoon and before the children get ready to go home. At Customs, children aged 5 are required to trace out simple Chinese characters and pinyins from the dotted prints and to write very simple ones only. Unfinished class assignments automatically become their homework. According to headteacher Chen, the teachers are not obliged to correct

Photo 22: Exercise books for writing Chinese ping-yin and Chinese characters

Photo 23: Exercise books for practising writing numbers and Chinese characters

Photo 24: Books for word recognition

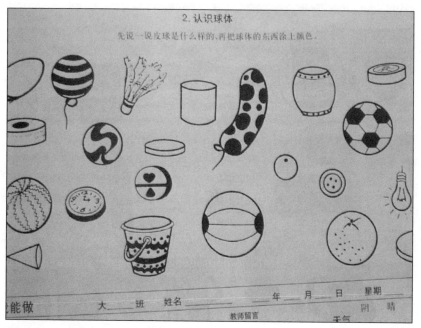

Photo 25: Worksheet on mathematical concepts

Photo 26: Teacher's sample of a clown's hat

Photo 27: Children's clown's hats

the children's assignments but some put a check mark or star on the finished work as an encouragement.

Sometimes children are required to make artwork which can be used to decorate the kindergarten and the entire period may be devoted to making handicrafts. The teachers will tell the children what to make, demonstrate how to make it, and show them the final product. They will encourage them to make it look different from other children's: for example, by designing the patterns differently and using different coloured papers. The kind of art work and materials used for artwork vary, depending on the teachers, as these photos show.

Photo 28: Teacher's example of a windmill

Photo 29: Children's windmills

Classroom environment and teaching resources

The furniture in the room is aligned in an orderly way with a piano and the children's desks on one side and learning centres on the other. During formal lesson time, the children are all seated. The centres are utilised once to twice a week during free activity time or when children have spare time (eg when waiting for others to finish lunch). The following photos show the various learning centres set up in the classrooms and the way teachers display the networking of concepts derived from a project on the walls.

The classroom is the main room for the children's activities but there are many areas affiliated to each classroom. So the children can enjoy a spacious learning environment which has been carefully designed to ensure healthy conditions, and encourage movement and involvement in activities.

The teachers use a combination of teaching resources such as commercial products (eg Montessori toys, Muppets, chess games) and dispensable materials (eg foam board, paper roll centres, bamboo sticks). The

Photo 30: A display of the project web on a classroom wall

Photo 31: Art centre and the mathematics centre

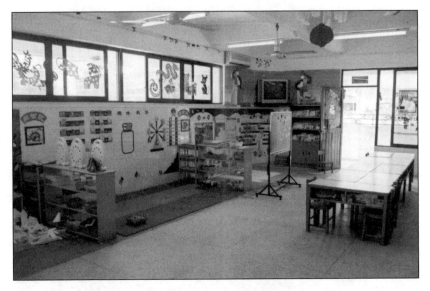

Photo 32: The language centre is at the corner near the entrance

green board, which can be wheeled around the room, and white chalk are the main tools for teaching and learning. Pictures can be pasted on the board during class discussions. Chinese pinyin, Chinese characters, mathematical concepts, and even drawing are essentially taught by using board and chalk.

Inner layer – the unique school culture

■ Customs Kindergarten is a dynamic school. With its emphasis on physical and mental health, it has created a physical environment which encourages a great deal of physical movement and exercise, while freeing the children of everyday constraints. Children are often seen scattered in the corridors, toilets, classrooms, bedroom or school bag room since the teachers do not expect total silence or absolute order at particular time. They speak to children in a friendly manner.

■ Even though Customs Kindergarten is not an elite school, it has a certain social and economic status and aims to provide the best possible conditions. The setting is designed to facilitate children's physical development. It is well staffed and the children are well fed and cared for.

■ The school is rather hierarchical. Teachers are delegated to play the roles of different leaders in school, eg leaders for classes of the same grade, leaders for each subject and two deputy heads, all under the headteacher.

■ Teaching is teacher-directed and learning is by means of demonstrations watched closely by the children. But they are also encouraged to distinguish their work from other children's. Teachers ask questions about the lesson and children are expected to provide original answers. The in-between-learning activities reflect that at Customs, every segment of time is used to include educational elements such as practising Chinese idioms, learning Chinese pinyin and Chinese characters. These in-between-learning activities also reflect that while the kindergarten is trying to adopt some Western pedagogical ideas, they are also trying to preserve the Chinese elements in the curriculum, although these have been marginalised as so little time is devoted to them. Some of these learning activities are scheduled in the afternoon sessions which are generally regarded as suitable for less important matters.

School culture and inter-relationships
The school and the children
Most children are from families with fairly high social and economical status. They are poised, eloquent, self-confident and display a rather broad knowledge base. Many live in the same neighbourhood, so their kindergarten is a familiar place. This familiarity may explain why they often wander around the corridors and bedroom. School life provides plenty of exercise, good food and care. Even though the lessons are teacher-led, children are encouraged to develop their own ideas after first following the teachers' instructions. Some children develop their ideas while others closely follow what the teachers have done or said.

The school and the teachers
The teachers are young, energetic, poised and confident. Their superiors have high expectation, of their personality and abilities. The two teachers in each class work as a team and those of the same grade also work closely together to discuss the progress of their projects and plan for outdoor activities and special events. As the teachers have to

handle a heavily loaded curriculum, there is little time for each subject in the curriculum. The parents are mostly well educated and expect the teachers to demonstrate professional knowledge in early childhood education. By the end of each term, their performance in teaching will be appraised through the children's performance evaluation.

So the teachers are busy, have long working hours, and shoulder numerous responsibilities, while trying to meet the expectations of their superiors. At the same time, there is a sense of community in their working environment.

The school and the parents

Since Kindergarten is considered as a welfare service for officers of the Customs Department, the teaching relationship with the parents is rather ambivalent. On the one hand, the parents are educated and feel at ease to comment on the curriculum and other aspects of the service. On the other hand, they are cooperative and generous when assistance is requested and they are willing to share the responsibility of educating their children. For instance, they will explore a certain topic with their children at home or bring in information about it. Some willingly visit the classrooms as guest speakers and teach children certain skills or knowledge. They are eager to find out about their children's development so participation at parent meetings and special events is high. All in all, the parents at Customs are educated and self-confident, and have high expectations of the kindergarten as well as their children.

Under their different social and educational systems, the two kindergartens are similar in some ways but not in others. While both attempt to implement a Western pedagogical strategy for their art work activities so as to promote children's creativity, the question is this: How does the borrowed pedagogy work in each of the two kindergartens? And what effect does the borrowed pedagogy have on the children? We move into the classroom settings in search of answers.

6

Progressive pedagogical strategies

Since the 1980s progressive pedagogical models (see Chapter 2) rooted in Western cultures have been adopted by kindergartens in both Macao and Zhuhai. In the last decade, interest has grown in the Reggio Emilia Programme from Italy and the Project Approach from the US. Teachers in Macao SAR and Zhuhai SER are now expected by their education authorities to foster children's creativity through innovative pedagogies. This expectation urges kindergartens to revise their programmes as well as their teaching approaches. Interestingly, the Project Approach is popular amongst kindergarten practitioners in Macao SAR and Zhuhai SER and has been adapted and experimented with by several kindergartens. The two public kindergartens have also tried to integrate this Western progressive pedagogy into their usual practice. The art work activities should provide readers with a fuller picture of how these Chinese kindergartens employ the Project Approach to foster children's creativity.

Preparations for the new pedagogy – Girassol Kindergarten

Before they started their new pedagogy based on the Project Approach, and now called Creative Teaching after the teachers had many meetings with one delegate from the Education and Youth Affairs Bureau and the headteacher for planning purposes. During morning circle time, class discussions are facilitated by the teachers' questioning, intended to stimulate the children's independent thinking. Each project takes roughly four weeks. To facilitate the new pedagogy, a new timetable modifies the afternoon sessions. Snack time in the original schedule (see

Chapter 5) is cancelled and one whole hour in the afternoon is reserved for construction activities, reflections and sharing ideas, and for children to evaluate their own performance that day. Subjects such as Portuguese, Chinese writing, mathematics, and sometimes worksheets are all finished or put away before nap time. Before the Creative Teaching was introduced, junk modelling and construction activities were not practised in these classrooms. Before each construction activity, the class teachers discuss with the children what they should do or observe their junk construction or art work activity. The routine is as follows:

- remind children about the theme of the activity as discussed that morning

- give children time to look for their partner(s), ie children group or re-group

- discuss whether they should work on something new or continue with unfinished work

- remind children of things to be careful about, such as not spilling water colour on the floor

- tell children about the resources prepared for them, such as photographs of different buildings and infrastructures in Macao SAR

- tell children about the kind of activities they can choose from – drawing, cutting pictures from magazines, reading, construction of object with junk materials

After this routine, the children quickly form into groups of twos, threes or fours. The class teachers will try to ensure that any who are on their own are accepted by a group by taking the child to the group they would like to join and persuading the group to accept them. If a child insists on working on their own, their wish is usually respected. The four middle points listed above are the result of the teachers' experiences and reflections on their problems and successes during the first two weeks of the experimental month. At first, the teachers did not issue many instructions or set many requirements but gave children 'maximum freedom' to work on their construction activities, individually or in groups. But because the teachers felt that the children were not learning much, they regulated the activities by following the points above.

Art work activities at Girassol Kindergarten

One of two construction activities videotaped at Girassol Kindergarten was on the project: Macao is My Home. The first project after the pilot was about the buildings and landmarks of Macao. The other was about Summer Time, where children made things to keep them cool in summer. The group was videotaped during the data analysis process trying to make an air-conditioner. Even athough these photos are not very sharp, they illustrate the essence of the activities.

'Macao is My Home' – constructing a mansion

When the construction activity resumed, the children retrieved their unfinished work from the day before and began working on it. A group of three or four had been using junk materials to build a mansion, its balconies, entrances, roof and windows. Each part of the mansion can be seen as a sub-goal of the whole. A large paper carton formed the body of the mansion. The children had drawn windows on the surface of the carton and attached small paper cartons to it to make entrances. At the beginning of the videotaping, they were trying to make a balcony out of pieces of cardboard.

One child (A) cut out a piece of cardboard, another (B) applied the scotch tape, and the third (C) held the cardboard in place while the others put the tape on. They did not find it easy. Child C says:

> *The scotch tape was too short.*

Child B takes this comment on board and applies more scotch tape to hold the pieces of cardboard together to create a balcony (Photo 33).

Then the children started to add more objects to the roof. Child A tried to secure a long cylindrical object (two paper roll centres joined to-

Photo 33: More scotch tape is applied to the balcony

Photo 34: Children switch roles

gether) to the roof of the mansion by placing it vertically on another object. As he was going to secure it with scotch tape, child C, who was watching, took the initiative to help by holding the upper part of the object so child A could apply scotch tape to the bottom part. Again, this was not an easy task. Then child A placed the cylindrical object on top of another object. This time child C, who had been silent throughout, tried to apply a piece of scotch tape to secure the cylindrical object and child A took his turn to be a helper (Photo 34).

Child B, who was watching all this, was ready to offer help. Child A was still unsuccessful. Child B took the object and put it on top of two paper roll centres that were already lying side by side each other, saying

Put it here.

Child A jokes about the three pieces of paper roll centres, as he happily put the piece of scotch tape he had been holding for a while on top of the three pieces (Photo 35):

Wow, is a baby born?

This time it works and child A remarks to child B:

You are quite smart.

Photo 35: Building on each other's ideas

Photo 36: Peers' social interaction

Then the three children each study the mansion again and attach more items to it. Child A does more work to the balconies while child B works on the entrance. Child A checks what child B would do next by asking him (Photo 36):

Hello, what are you doing?

Meanwhile, child C is adding more film containers to the roof. While he is struggling to get a piece of scotch tape from the dispenser, Vong *sin san* approaches him, squats beside him and shows him how to make use of the scotch tape dispenser once, then helps him to pull out a piece. By the time this piece is cut halfway through, the teacher has let go and the child completes the task alone and picks up the piece of scotch tape.

Child C wanted to put the piece of scotch tape onto the lid of a plastic film container, but the two were already tightly attached. Vong *sin san* asks him whether any scotch tape was needed to secure the lid of the film container to its body. When child C seems to understand why it was unnecessary, Vong *sin san* lets him continue with his work.

Photo 37: Teacher helping a child to use the scotch tape dispenser

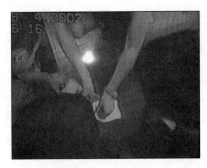

Photo 38: Teacher supports children's work by playing the role of an assistant

Towards the end of the construction time, children A and B try to make the regional flag and put it on the roof. Lo *sin san* comes by and helps them by holding the straw (supposedly the flagpole) in place and lets the children tape it to the paper flag on which the logo was already drawn (Photo 38).

When it was put up, Lo *sin san* cheered,

'Bravo'.

To wrap up the construction time, all the children had to sit on the carpet where they had morning lessons and, group by group, they presented their work to the whole class and received applause from their audience (Photo 39).

Constructing an air-conditioner for 'Summer Time' project

After the warm-up routines, the children started to work on their own or in groups. The group I videotaped looked through the information (photos, drawings, charts) the teachers provided and decided to make an air-conditioner. They kept looking at the one on the wall and discussed it for a while.

Photo 39: Children presenting and reflecting about their construction

Photo 40: Teacher and children planning together

Three children (a girl and two boys, one of whom was child A in the previous project) got a thick rectangular paper carton and Vong *sin san* sat on the floor and discussed with them what they could do with the materials (Photo 40).

Vong sin san:	*What do you want to do now?*
Child A:	*We want to make an air-conditioner (pointing to the one up on the wall).*
Vong sin san:	*What colour?*
Child A:	*White.*
Vong sin san:	*Let's try to make a more real one. We've used white before. This time, let's make a more real one (pointing to the same air-conditioner). What are we going to make it with?*
Child A:	*White paper.*
Vong sin san:	*White paper. Are there any small openings on the white paper?*
All three children:	*No (shaking their heads).*
Vong sin san:	*No. When you worked on 'Macao is My Home' last time...*
Child A:	*(interrupts) Can cut it open.*
Vong sin san:	*Yes, can cut it open. Try to make a more real one. Last time, you pasted paper on things...*

(realising that another group is about to work on some materials, she turns to them and asks them to wait as she would like to discuss what they should do before they start. Then she continues her sentence.)

	Now, take some time to study the air-conditioner (pointing to it). Look at it, try to make a more real one.
Child A:	*But last time I used the cutter, I hurt my finger.*
Vong sin san:	*I'll help you.*
Child D:	*We can use the scissors to cut it open.*
Vong sin san:	*That's right (pointing and gesturing on the paper carton). Use a cutter to make an opening first. Cut a small part, then like what he said, use what?*
Child A:	*Scissors.*
Vong sin san:	*Yes, then use scissors to cut it open. Scissors are less dangerous.*
Child A:	*Scissors can cut along the paper carton.*
Vong sin san:	*That's right.*

The three children then started to work on the paper carton with scissors. Child A did the cutting while the girl, who had been silent, held the paper carton to facilitate the cutting. But the paper carton was thick and hard. Child A observed:

It's difficult to cut it open.

Child D, who had been observing the cutting process, at once offered help by putting his hand on child A's and the two small hands worked on the cutting together until it was done (Photo 41).

Photo 41: Peers helping each other

Preparations for the new pedagogy – Customs Kindergarten

At Customs Kindergarten, the ideas of the Project Approach have been integrated into the curriculum of two classes of 5-year-olds from the beginning of the term. Beforehand, the Customs teachers had either visited kindergartens in another Chinese city which had been experimenting with the Project Approach, or had watched the videos they had made. A project normally lasts for two weeks but only about 30 minutes of the main lesson time in the morning is devoted to project discussions. The teachers have to handle other domains of learning as well and each has a specific set of requirements and teaching objectives, for example,

- in music, there is music appreciation, songs, dancing, rhythmic music

- in language, there is Chinese pinyin, writing of Chinese characters, recognition of Chinese characters, poems and rhymes

Each domain is handled independently through the week and the content does not have to relate to the project. Artwork activities at Customs Kindergarten comprise traditional Chinese art such as paper cutting, paper folding and other art forms such as fruit carving, collage and simple handicrafts using two dimensional materials. Junk modelling and construction were not valued at Customs until after the Project Approach and the Reggio Emilia Programme gained attention in mainland China. Under these Western influences, art work activities are now considered beneficial for children's creativity. Two or three afternoons a week are reserved for art work.

Two artwork activities at Customs Kindergarten

For one of the artwork activities, children were given foam board (cut into various sizes and shapes), toothpicks and bamboo sticks to make animals or other objects. The other K3 class made pen holders. Both classes were also working on a project on Buildings, but the classes did not have to work on the same topic for art work. In the first class, the children watched how the teacher made an animal with the foam boards. Then they were given the materials, tools and time to produce their foam board animals. Again, the photos are produced for the purpose of data analysis.

Making animals from foam board

Zhong *lao shi* (*lao shi* is teacher in Mandarin) started by dividing the class into two. One group stayed in the classroom and sat around a large rectangular table formed by putting the desks together, while the other went into the corridor for some kind of a drawing activity with the assistant teacher, Ding *lao shi*. Then the two teachers swapped groups so keeping the child to teacher ratio low.

When the group in the class was seated, Zhong *lao shi* stood in front of them and demonstrated how to join the pieces of foam board together by inserting toothpicks as joints to make the different parts of an animal. She used a round piece for the head and two square pieces for the ears of an elephant. Then she attached a long rectangular piece to the round one to make the trunk, explaining to the class what she was doing as she went along.

Zhong lao shi:	*(While she is still in action) And we can make the trunk tilt upwards.*
Zhong lao shi:	*How about this? Do you think it looks like an elephant? If you don't think so, you can use a shorter piece to make the trunk. And then, what else, we can make a big and fat, what?*
Children:	*Body.*
Zhong lao shi:	*Yes (while she adds a square piece below the round one to make the body and looks for two short rectangular pieces for the front and hind legs).*
Zhong lao shi:	*When you find the leg and what?*
Children:	*Hand (front leg).*
Zhong lao shi:	*Hand. Both are possible. You join them to the body and you will turn it into, what?*
Children:	*An elephant.*
Zhong lao shi:	*An elephant, but it's just one side of it. There is another side (while she continues to finish the attachments). Let's see who can make the prettiest one.*

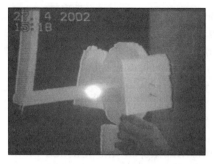

Photo 42: Teacher shows children her finished work

When the elephant was completed (Photo 42), Zhong *lao shi* invited the children to make other animals or things.

Then Zhong *lao shi* covered the desks with a piece of blue cloth to turn it into a large work table. On it she put baskets of bamboo sticks and a pile of foam board (Photo 43).

Before the activity, Zhong *lao shi* stressed that each child should work on their own. She placed baskets of bamboo sticks and a pile of foam board on the work table.

Even though the children were allowed to make different animals and other things, all made animals and many made elephants. When a girl had finished making an elephant, Zhong *lao shi* examined the elephant and commented on it (Photo 44).

> Zhong lao shi: *Children, look here. This is a finished elephant.*
> *Even though Zhong lao shi thinks it's very pretty*
> *and resembles the real one. But it's not perfect.*
> *Let's add some decorations to it. (Zhong lao shi*

Photo 43: Children seated along the work table waiting for the teacher to get materials ready

Photo 44: Teacher demonstrates how to add decorations while a child pays close attention to her instructions

85

> *began to insert a line of toothpick to the head of*
> *the elephant.) This is the elephant's hair. (She then*
> *inserted toothpicks to the front leg of the*
> *elephant.) And these are the elephant's fingers.*

After this brief demonstration, the children started to insert toothpicks into the different body parts of their animals. It was about time to clean up for the next activity and Zhong *lao shi* helped some children finish their work by taking over. When time was up, all the finished foam board animals were displayed on the cupboard (Photo 45).

Making pen holders

Zhou *lao shi* was in charge of this activity in a K3 class and set out scissors, self-adhesive coloured paper, paper roll centres. The whole class participated in this activity so the other teacher and caretaker were there ready to offer assistance to children.

Zhou *lao shi* stood in front of the whole class and demonstrated how to make a pen holder with the tools and materials available. First, she covered the surface of a small paper roll centre, intended to be the cover of the pen holder, with a piece of oversized rectangular self-adhesive paper.

Zhou lao shi:	*Alright. It's a bit too much. What should we do?*
Child:	*Cut it off.*
Zhou lao shi:	*That's right. Think of a solution. Take a pair of scissors and cut it open, then... (she begins to cut the edge of the oversized self-adhesive paper into fringes)* (Photo 46)

Photo 45: Children's work on display

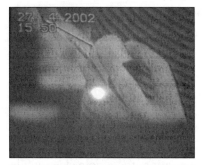

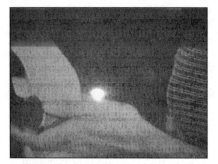

Photo 46: Teacher demonstrates how to cut something open

Photo 47: Teacher demonstrates how to remove a piece of back-up paper

Child:	*Tuck it (the fringes) in.*
Zhou lao shi:	*That's right. Wrap it (the paper roll centre) up. Is it very convenient? (Then Zhou lao shi tucks the redundant self-adhesive paper inwards so that the edge of the paper roll centre is wrapped). Alright, the cover of my small pen holder is finished.*

Using the same pedagogical strategy, Zhou *lao shi* covered the surface of the body of the pen holder.

Zhou lao shi:	*But we have to measure how much paper we need. How to measure? (Without waiting for the children to answer, she is already doing it) Can you see how teacher measures it? Go around once. Wow, so much is left. Don't waste material, cut it off. Now teacher is going to paste it. Do we need to remove the back-up paper from the self-adhesive paper all at once?*
Children:	*No.*
Zhou lao shi:	*That's right. Just open it up a little bit. Put the paper roll centre on the self-adhesive paper along the edge and as you go along, remove the back-up paper bit by bit, otherwise, it's difficult to paste it flat on the paper roll centre (Photo 47).*
One of the children:	*Or it will all wrinkle up.*
Zhou lao shi:	*Right. Look, did I do a good job?*

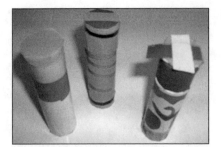

Photo 48: Children's work on display

When Zhou *lao shi* had finished demonstrating, the whole class, while still sitting at their own seats, were given the same tools and materials to make their own pen holder and encouraged to choose the colour they liked and design patterns on the self-adhesive paper when the pen holder was done. Not many children had completed making their pen holder by the end of the session so they were allowed to finish it at home. All the finished pen holders were displayed on shelf (Photo 48).

Distinct schools and pedagogies and unique features

The art work activities observed demonstrate that while each pedagogical approach has its own characteristics, they stem from the same Chinese traditions of teaching and learning, and both are contriving to construct a creative pedagogy.

Both kindergartens attempt to integrate the Project Approach into their pedagogical approaches. But Girassol Kindergarten appears more flexible in its scheduling and time is allowed to make the most of the art work activities such as allocating time for thinking, discussion, practise and evaluation. At Girassol, the teachers' discussions and reflections on the questioning techniques and effectiveness of each project facilitate the implementation of the next one. And there is a generous supply of materials for junk construction.

At Customs Kindergarten, each art work activity is limited to 30 minutes and each is seen as an individual task. Also, the teachers' energy is diverted to other domains of children's learning valued in the curriculum. Even though the teachers work in pairs and groups to plan for the main project lessons and art work activities, these are not planned or organised as a whole, so the children's learning seems rather fragmented. The supply of materials and resources is limited to what the teachers assigned for use.

88

Girassol Kindergarten has set a wider stage for implementing their new pedagogy. The four art work activities illustrated here have already revealed some of the complexities in the transformational process. Due to the different social and cultural ecological contexts, the transplanted pedagogy appears rather differently in each kindergarten.

7

Chinese practitioners' perspectives
on the new pedagogies

I n 1989, Tobin, Wu and Davidson published a study of the social changes in Japan, China and America by studying preschool practices. These researchers gained insights from the different ways in which the function of preschool education were viewed and attributed the disparities they found to the cultural beliefs and ethos of each society. As they suggested, preschools both reflect and affect social change: they are complex institutions embedded in communities, nations and cultures.

I adapted the multi-vocal method from Tobin *et al* and after my video recordings were completed, the teaching staff in Macao SAR and Zhuhai SER who had dedicated roles and with whom the 5 to 6-year-olds had frequent contact, were invited to watch four video-recorded episodes and then respond to open-ended questions in semi-structured interviews. That is, the practitioners from each of the two kindergartens were invited to comment on their own as well as their counterparts' pedagogy in terms of learning and cognition. These insiders' responses were also recorded, fully transcribed and the key questions translated and reported. Towards the end of this chapter, the different perspectives from the two kindergartens are drawn together in order to identify both the shared and disparate views.

The primary purpose of this study is to learn from the participants their opinions of certain educational issues and how they construct their pedagogy accordingly. This phenomenological perspective reflects their beliefs and psychological constructs. While there is a need to organise the discourses so as to make sense of implied local knowledge, I have tried to preserve their meaning so they are clear. The Macao teachers' comments on five issues are presented first.

Girassol Kindergarten in Macao SAR
How learning and cognition are interpreted
The headteacher and two class teachers all mention that imitating or following others in what they do is learning, although they are aware that this is not a new idea. For instance,

Headteacher Leung: *narrowly speaking, to understand, to comprehend something given to us... imitation, such as doing exactly the same as others, it could be learning*

Vong sin san: *we imitate the past, ... knowledge comes from books of people in the past*

Lo sin san: *follow other ... it's like the old saying ... learning is a kind of manipulation, then you see something, then you want to follow how he does it, then you do it, it's a kind of learning*

It is clear that the participants' understanding of learning is drawn from the past and that this remains an important part of their present understanding of learning. Lo *sin san* put it succinctly,

Lo sin san: *schooling in the past, that is, the teacher read one sentence, children read one sentence, that's also learning*

Comments on the two new pedagogical approaches
These teachers are quick to realise the role of demonstration or modelling in the approach adopted by their counterparts at Customs Kindergarten. They consider such strategies to be traditional.

Vong sin san: *they give the children a style to do things, ... children can have some changes, ... but a certain model has been given to them first, so that's somewhat traditional*

Headteacher Leung says that at Customs Kindergarten children's thinking is constrained by the teachers' pedagogical strategies.

> *Headteacher Leung:*   *teachers will do things on behalf of those who do not know how ... the materials available are limited...*
>
> *the materials are already fixed and provided for children who do not have to think ... or use their thinking on choosing materials*

The headteacher realised that the classroom activities at Customs Kindergarten allowed for little social interaction as there was little communication between the children or with teachers.

> *Headteacher Leung:*   *there is little communication between teacher and children ...there is no communication amongst the children*

The Girassol teachers characterised their own approach by its openness and suggested a relationship between openness and children's learning. From the pedagogy of their counterparts, Lo *sin san* recognised the changes in their own.

> *Lo sin san:*   *our approach is more advanced, because ... we just let them do things ... they have to demonstrate ...that is like what we did before we employ the project approach*

Lo *sin san*'s comments and my observations of their art work activities before the experimental period show that the Girassol teachers' pedagogy was similar to that observed at Customs before the art work activities were video-taped.

The headteacher highlighted the opportunities for collaboration that children at her kindergarten have in those classroom activities:

> *Headteacher Leung:*   *... in the process, teachers will talk to children about what they are doing ... there are lots of opportunities for children to interact*

Although both the headteacher and the researcher do not regard demonstration as an important aspect in this pedagogy, Vong *sin san* expressed her stance on modelling, which she considers as something necessary for children's learning.

> Vong sin san: *but teachers have to demonstrate at the appropriate time, it's impossible to make children learn all by themselves from their experiences – there are things that need to be taught to them first*

Lo *sin san* does not question this and it seems that at least some teachers at Girassol still regard demonstration as a necessary teaching strategy and will use it when it is needed.

Views on what supports learning

The Girassol teachers thought that at both kindergartens, the teachers' involvement in the learning process provided a strong incentive and inspiration for the children to keep thinking and learning.

> Headteacher Leung: *in both kindergartens, the teachers give children a starting point for further thinking, and freedom in doing things*

> Vong sin san: *it's the teachers' continuous guidance,... the issue lies in the difference in our role ... learning is not about children learning on their own*

They also considered that the children's interest in the activity and product was a supportive aspect for their learning.

> Headteacher Leung: *the interest in what they are doing will support children's learning ... the product that they are making propels their learning.*

Interestingly, Lo *sin san* suggests that even though teachers demonstrate and children imitate at Customs Kindergarten, the children have opportunities for further thinking that supports their learning.

> Lo sin san: *the process of brain storming ... in the process, when imitating, he thinks of something else to make, ... he is in fact thinking.*

Again, the role of imitation, and therefore teachers' demonstrations, is considered important for children's learning. Learning is not believed to be independent of teachers' guidance and sometimes explicit demonstrations are needed.

The abilities developed by the pedagogies

All three participants agree that both of the new approaches allow children's abilities to develop. However, the kinds of abilities developed are not the same. The children at Customs Kindergarten mainly develop various technical skills and some general knowledge through activities, for example:

> Lo sin san: *the skill of using self-adhesive colour paper ... and realise that toothpicks can be used with foam boards*

The Girassol teachers assert that children trained under their new pedagogy, on the other hand, develop a broader range of abilities such as various social skills, technical skills and abstract thinking.

> Vong sin san: *interact with other children ... and the skill to hold scissors, to apply scotch tape*

> Lo sin san: *there is more creative thinking on the Macao side ... searching for information that they do not know, ... it's a skill*

The headteacher believes that their new pedagogy enhances the children's language, especially their ability to critique their own work and that of others', due to the reflective aspect of the activities.

> Headteacher Leung: *after making their things, there is literacy involved and, group analysis ... they know how to ... learn to ... critique*

Values of the two pedagogies

Discussing the values of the two approaches is a sensitive matter. Head-teacher Leung and Lo *sin san* are confident in saying that their approach is more valuable and effective in children's learning. But they have different reasons for their stance.

> Headteacher Leung: *I think ours is more valuable ... there are extended activities and children's interest is getting more intense because after these activities, there is something connected to their everyday life*

> Lo sin san: *our approach is more effective or valuable, self-initiation is strong*

However, Vong *sin san* takes additional perspectives into account. She clearly delineates the pros and cons of each of the two pedagogical approaches and expresses concern about the discrepancies in the children's skills and cognitive development.

> *Vong sin san:*   *in Zhuhai, they have many students, so their*
> *approach makes children's progress more even ...*
> *our approach suits small classes, for those who*
> *only wander around in the classroom, teachers*
> *can guide them more, ... otherwise ... he, we do not*
> *know what he has done for the whole day ... our*
> *approach is less boring ... but whether their skills*
> *can be ensured or not, varies from child to child*

According to Vong *sin san*, the pedagogy currently employed by teachers at Customs, although full of demonstrations and imitations, also has value. Under this pedagogy, children's basic skills and knowledge is more solid, more uniform – especially when it is a big class – and teachers' influence is more certain. A more open-ended pedagogy requires many conditions to fully support children's learning in terms of the pace of progress and solidity of the skills and knowledge being developed. In fact, Vong *sin san* has raised the concerns of many Chinese teachers facing a high teacher-child ratio.

Customs Kindergarten at Zhuhai SER

The following sections examine the Customs Kindergarten teachers' understanding of children's learning and cognition in relation to the two new pedagogical approaches. The five issues discussed above are also considered in the semi-structured interviews conducted at the kindergarten. The responses to questions 1 and 5 are treated in the same way as for Girassol Kindergarten teachers. Altogether, I interviewed nine participants: headteacher Chen, four class teachers, three interest group teachers, one science teacher.

Understanding of learning
Responses from these interviewees revealed four key ideas about what learning means. First, the meaning of the term has changed over time and there is a tendency to pay more attention to the process of learning than the results. For instance,

Headteacher Chen: *in the traditional concept, learning means he imitates what I say, that's learning, teachers teach, children learn, all is about imitation ... I draw a picture and you draw one that's exactly the same, that's traditional learning ... now, it's about innovation, breaking the restrictions of Chinese education, advocate creativeness, or children innovate ... now learning is about independence, creativeness and autonomy*

Zhang lao shi: *it's training, learning things; in the past, there is more emphasis on the result ... now there is relatively more emphasis on the process, in the process, manifest that, that, that kind of thought which expresses oneself, and also, those experiences, ... relatively emphasise on the experiences or what they see and hear*

Second, learning was understood as the process of absorbing stimulation or information from the environment. This concept of learning implies that learning is a result of interactions between an individual and their environment, without considering the social aspects of learning. These interpretations of learning are in line with the constructivists' idea of children's learning, which places less emphasis upon social aspects of the process. For example:

Ding lao shi: *look at your environment, by looking, listening, talking, whatever sorts of – all sorts of – channels are there*

Dance teacher: *learning is a conditional reflex ... I think the beginning of learning is like this ... not only the teacher, the surrounding environment can have an influence on you ... it's like dancing, ... you can read some books, look at some VCDs, discover from them, there is also learning*

Third, imitation is considered a key factor in learning because it is a means to learn and practice. There is evidence that even though some teachers regard learning by following what teachers do as traditional practice, others wish to still uphold this tradition.

Art teacher:	*'xue xi' (Chinese term for learning) is separated ... xue is to follow what the teacher does, xi is to practise, the process of repeatedly practise until skillful*
English teacher:	*I also think that 'xue' comes from the teacher or on the basis of absorbing from the physical environment, then comes learning, then 'xi' should not be simply understood as practise repeatedly ... I think that 'xi' is, 'xi' is to gain a concept, to gain an idea*
Science teacher:	*following others is a kind of learning*

Although the crucial role of imitation and practise are emphasised by the interest group teachers, it is not mentioned by the class teachers who employ demonstration in their pedagogy. This might suggest that even though there have been some conceptual changes in teachers' ideas about learning, they still rely unconsciously on demonstrations and explicit instructions in their teaching.

Fourth, learning is also the process of knowing what one does not know or improving one's cognition.

Ding lao shi:	*through this learning, this process, [we] acquire things that one doesn't know or improve them even further, or improve oneself, improve from the original foundations*
Science teacher:	*from not knowing to knowing*

These responses indicate that there is still no consensus on the meaning of learning amongst these teachers. Learning appears to be a matter of acquiring or accumulating knowledge and abilities, whether through imitating other people, spontaneously picking up information from the environment, or experiencing different possibilities in the process.

Comments on the new pedagogies

According to their reading of their own pedagogy, the mainland teachers thought that demonstration plays different roles in children's learning, in particular, laying down foundations before allowing children to develop their ideas.

Zhou lao shi:	Zhong lao shi and I both give demonstrations ... at least the basic ways to manipulate ... then that – that – exterior shape, exterior colour, and patterns etc. can be drawn or designed by them
Ding lao shi:	our teachers demonstrate, progress layer by layer
English teacher:	our side is simply to finish it on one's own, first the teacher demonstrates how to manipulate

Another obvious characteristic of the pedagogy at Customs is its emphasis on training children's technical skills, which form the foundations of their learning.

Art teacher:	this side is more of a kind of training in skills ... ours belongs to a kind of foundational lesson to train skills

The teachers defined different kinds of restrictions on children's thinking and these can be attributed directly to the teacher's role. The interest group teachers were more open about acknowledging those restrictions than the class teachers themselves.

Ding lao shi:	our teachers, they step by step, layer their teaching
Dance teacher:	ours is teacher-oriented
English teacher:	everything accords to her concept, fixing children to that thinking in no time, it's very difficult for children to give free rein again ... I still feel that children on this side are constrained

It is worth noting that Zhong lao shi's foam board activity is regarded as an acceptable approach by herself as well as by many of her colleagues. Despite her demonstrations and explanations, she still allows room for individual thinking.

Headteacher Chen:	the two teachers are not totally traditional ... autonomy is partially given ... the teachers have given a little space to the reform
Zhong lao shi:	then it's me, mine is a bit loose ... I make something casually ... then I let children do it by themselves

99

English teacher: *the space to imagine given to children by Zhong lao shi's lesson, is still smaller than that in Macao, but it's greater than Zhou lao shi's lesson*

It seems that the respondents expect teachers to allow room and 'freedom' for children to develop their own ideas and thinking so as to meet the expectations of the undergoing reform. The class teachers say that implementating a less restrictive pedagogy is made difficult by the many constraints in their daily teaching.

Zhou lao shi: *our side ... this kind of manipulative activity is relatively fewer ... there are so many other things to be done, even for art itself. There are paper cutting, paper folding, collage, drawing, art appreciation, handicrafts, etc*

Zhang lao shi: *on our side ... time for hands on manipulation is comparatively less than theirs*

Dance teacher: *there are objective reasons, too many children*

As for the pedagogy practised at Girassol Kindergarten, Customs teachers saw freedom, autonomy and independence as being clearly evident in its classroom activities.

Headteacher Chen: *I appreciate the activity in Macao very much, it's relaxed, autonomous, and children are joyous and free ... teacher's role is well played, do not demonstrate, or interfere children, do not explain, do not give children a frame ... activity shows children's autonomy, show their creativeness ... the activity in Macao is closer to the advocated reform, liberate children, give free rein to their autonomy, creativeness*

Ding lao shi: *their teachers only supervise them on the side ... there is freedom, free to create, free to give free rein*

Art teacher: *children's dependence on teachers is much smaller, autonomy is strong, ... basically they are very independent*

As well as the autonomy and independence the children enjoy, peer collaboration is also recognised as a key characteristic of the Girassol approach.

Zhang lao shi: *there is relatively more collaboration, I think they emphasise that kind of collaboration*

Art teacher: *it's a group creation, pulling everyone's thoughts together and to create, on our side, this training is in fact, lacking*

Science teacher: *the best aspect is that it's collaborative work, because now they are the only child, as far as social development goes, the macro environment is not good ... foster their cooperativeness, interacting with other people, coordinating, it's well manifested ... the Macao side manifests collaboration and sufficient space for imagination, it's immense, ... there is manifestation of their collective wisdom*

These teachers thought that besides being free and independent, the classroom activities at Girassol showed signs of openness and space for children's thinking to develop.

Headteacher Chen: *the space to diverge (thinking) is immense*

Zhang lao shi: *on Macao side, it seems that they emphasise relatively more on thinking of a way, how to do it better, this may mean that the children can open up even more*

Zhong lao shi: *it's a kind of open approach*

Some of the Customs teachers were impressed that the approach employed at Girassol Kindergarten encourages children to be imaginative and creative.

Headteacher Chen: *it encourages using objects for objects, using different kinds of junk materials, develops children's creativity*

| Art teacher: | *teachers leave the materials lying around casually, children rely on their imagination to place these things, to give free rein to imagination, to put to somewhere suitable* |

Although not recognised as a key characteristic, the approach at Girassol Kindergarten also develops technical skills, acquired not through modelling but through the activities themselves.

| Dance teacher: | *when children are doing hands-on activities, they will discover the things they don't know, then ask for help right away. I like it* |
| English teacher: | *the approach to teach during an activity makes it easier for children to accept, ... and it's not easy to forget* |

These responses indicate that most mainland Chinese teachers show more appreciation of the pedagogy practised by Girassol Kindergarten than that in their own classrooms because of the space, freedom and autonomy in thinking and working the Girassol children enjoy.

Views on what supports learning

According to the Customs teachers, the key factor which sustains their pupils' learning is the teachers' style of teaching and their roles in the classroom, such as being a classroom monitor and an admirer of the children's work.

Headteacher Chen:	*for our side, they sit for so long, maybe they have grown up and there is a desire to learn, or comply with the disciplines ... maybe it's a kind of consciousness of rules*
Zhou lao shi:	*then there is teachers' requirement, children's mutual influence*
Zhong lao shi:	*then, in the process, ... maybe teachers' praises are needed*

The sense of achievement of children at Customs does support their learning at Customs Kindergarten.

Zhou lao shi:	I also feel that it's the sense of achievement which supports their learning
Zhang lao shi:	there is satisfaction upon completion of a product

Various factors are identified as supportive to children's learning at Girassol. First, it is the children's interest in the activities that motivates their learning. Then there is the sense of achievement they derive from the activities.

Headteacher Chen:	it's the kind of interest ... they know Macao quite well, they see lots of materials, and the activity is so free, so open
Zhang lao shi:	in both cases, it's children's interest, these handicrafts are activities children are interested in
Zhou lao shi:	I also feel that it's the sense of achievement which supports their learning
Zhong lao shi:	maybe their own little achievement is relatively attractive ... then at the end, there is evaluation, everyone applauds
Zhang lao shi:	children's interest, and there is satisfaction upon completion of a product

The mainland teachers associated two characteristics with the pedagogy practised at Girassol but not at Customs Kindergarten. One of these is peer collaboration, as these comments illustrate:

Zhang lao shi:	then there is collaboration
Art teacher:	some children like to do things independently ... meaning they have paid attention to this point, let them choose according to their own choice
Science teacher:	there is a desire to manifest Macao through hands-on manipulation and everyone's collaboration

The second are the kinds of simulated real-life activities which appear to form a driving force for children's learning.

Zhong lao shi:	*in Macao, it's relatively closer to reality, the theme is ... there is a close relationship with modern society, making children want to create*
Science teacher:	*at Macao, it's relatively more real, closer to reality, and materials are rich and from everyday life*

So these mainland teachers are of the view that the teachers' roles (monitoring and praising the children's work) and the children's intrinsic satisfaction (sense of achievement) gained through their activities are the main factors which support children's learning at Customs. On the other hand, the driving forces or supportive aspects of Girassol Kindergarten come either from the children's sense of achievement, interest and the connection they build between an activity and their daily life or from social aspects such as teachers' praise, and collaboration amongst the children. Interestingly, these mainland Chinese teachers do not consider the Girassol teachers' continuous guidance as a crucial aspect in supporting children's learning.

Abilities developed under the two pedagogies

The Customs teachers are clear that their approach can foster children's technical skills.

Zhang lao shi:	*they've learned some skills––- such as cutting, pasting, threading, inserting, and those shapes, and ... how to make something stand upright*
Science teacher:	*Zhou lao shi's lesson is solely training some basic hands-on skills ... those drawing, drawing the circle, cutting ... in the foam board activity, the main thing is the skill to put together and insert the toothpicks ... Zhou lao shi's lesson manifests the children's skills in collage.*

These mainland teachers recognise that their pupils have also developed some basic knowledge about animals and mathematical concepts through their classroom activities.

Zhou lao shi:	*there is also knowledge, for example, ... there is colour, and then – pattern designs, then, ... how to set the shape of an animal*

Dance teacher:	*the different shapes of animals ... understand animals' exterior characteristics, it's within cognitive development*
Science teacher:	*the most obvious development is the process of moving from two- to three-dimensional kinds of activity, developing children's thinking about solid objects ... their understanding of cylindrical objects*

The Customs teachers described the abilities and knowledge displayed by the Girassol staff as an integrated ability. They saw the approach practised at Girassol as fostering creativeness and imagination in the children, and also collaboration.

Headteacher Chen:	*what they've learned are integrated abilities such as how to coordinate, how to work together, how to replace objects with objects [eg using a bottle to make a telephone booth], which involves their brain, how to use materials, and the space for imagination is large*
Dance teacher:	*on the Macao side, their integrated training of abilities is stronger ... their training brings in the old and new abilities*
Science teacher:	*the lesson in Macao manifests an integrated ability to cut, paste, construct, put together, apply tools ... there is also a kind of emotional release, and fostering of children's feeling for their homeland*
Headteacher Chen:	*the approach in Macao is suitable for fostering people of a new style, ... children have creativeness, and can use materials smartly and with the spirit to collaborate*
Zhang lao shi:	*the collaboration on Macao side is especially strong, ... then there is the social side, those mutual discussions for solutions ... I also think that the space to imagine is greater*

Science teacher: *preparation of resources, because there is plenty,*
                    children's selection is relatively wider, ... so their
                    capacity for imagination is great ... the biggest
                    development is to develop children's ability to
                    collaborate because social development and
                    collaborating with peers are important in
                    kindergartens, it's a manifestation of quality
                    education

So the Customs teachers think that the pedagogical approach employed by their Macao counterparts can foster broader abilities in children, as manifested through the art work activities.

The values of the two pedagogies

The responses to this question were mixed. Some teachers prefer the pedagogical approach practised at Girassol to their own because they believe that it can build children's autonomy, minimise imitation, yet reinforce children's collaboration and opportunities for imaginative and creative thinking.

Headteacher Chen: *I think the approach in Macao meets the standard*
                    of an activity ... I consider is that children are
                    strong in autonomy, they are relaxed and joyous,
                    interested, and the teacher can activate all his
                    abilities or passion, or develop his creative
                    thinking ... to do something

Zhang lao shi: *I also feel that the approach of Macao is better ...*
                    for the things I talked about just now

Science teacher: *their activity is better, ... you see the things [they]*
                    make] are rich in imagination, objects are used for
                    objects, and look so real, and then it's obvious that
                    they are passionate about their place, and the
                    regional flag is made

However, quite a few respondents would like to see a combination of the two approaches, blending basic skills training with the openness for thinking. The Customs teachers echo a Girassol teacher in their concern that the children's technical skill is built on solid foundations.

Ding lao shi:	*both have their own characteristics ... taking points from each teacher would be most effective ... for example, take the step by step approach of Zhong lao shi, then take the boldness of Macao teachers*
Art teacher:	*that's the kind of reform, it's a road of blending, and not giving up one side*
English teacher:	*I cannot say which educational approach is better ... the two sides should combine together, if we let children do whatever they want and on their own, they may do something different every day, then what he has learned will not be solid*

Thus some of the respondents favour blending the two kinds of teaching, but they see the two pedagogies observed as quite disparate while still believing that the two strategies could be fused.

Similarities and differences in the teachers' perspectives

The participating practitioners' responses to the open-ended questions suggest that their interpretations of children's learning and cognition are complex, as the foci of their educational ideas sometimes vary but at other times coincide. The key similarities and differences are outlined below.

- Practitioners at both kindergartens share the idea that imitation, although a traditional concept, is a distinct aspect of learning, while the Customs teachers also articulate interpretations of learning which appear to stem from Western theories.

- A general consensus among the teachers from both schools is that the pedagogy at Customs Kindergarten is characterised by demonstration, whereas openness, autonomy, and the space for thinking are more noticeable at Girassol. However, many teachers at Customs regard demonstration and modelling as a fundamental step in children's learning. Interestingly, one teacher at Girassol agrees, but with the difference that she thinks demonstration should be used only when necessary.

- Teachers at both kindergartens identified more supportive elements in children's art work activities at Girassol Kindergarten, such as children's interest in the simulated real-life activities, their sense of achievement, teachers' encouragement and, more importantly, peer collaboration amongst the children. But the value of the Girassol teachers' continual guidance during the process is not recognised by the mainland Chinese teachers.

- The general opinion in both is that Girassol can foster integrated abilities in children which are not acquired through direct demonstration and imitation, while Customs can develop children's skills and basic knowledge through the demonstration and imitation process.

- It is clear that most of the teachers claim that the pedagogy at Girassol Kindergarten is preferable as it offers children more opportunities to develop abstract thinking which uses their imagination and creativity, while peer collaboration is not sacrificed. But some teachers still consider that building a good foundation for children's later development through step by step demonstrations and direct instructions is important too.

These local perspectives on children's learning and cognition show that the practitioners have both conventional and non-conventional Chinese educational ideas which they might or might not put into practice. Old ideas and new all play a part in the practitioners' construction of a new pedagogy which might be recognised by the practitioners. Their educational ideas are bound to affect their understanding of creativity: what works and what doesn't work in fostering creativity in children. The next chapter brings the expectations of the governments onto the scene.

8
Chinese practitioners' views about creativity

Howard Gardner's accounts of the social and educational scenarios of mainland China in the late 1980s are based on his experience of school visits and personal conversations with Chinese educators. He notes the special position of creativity within the Chinese education system, which places emphasis upon imitation, upon product rather than process, on the role of the teacher rather than the child, and on the centralisation of content and basic skill development in learning (Gardner, 1989:15, 248, 250). Since Gardner's visit to China in the 1980s, the country has undergone immense political, social and economic change. The Open Door Policy encourages exchanges of educational ideas with other parts of the world, thus creating a platform for more educational reform in mainland China. Thus the concept of creativity for contemporary Chinese teachers is likely to have changed.

Chapter 4 reviewed the different definitions of creativity in the official documents of Macao SAR and mainland China as well as those of Western and Chinese scholars and practitioners. With no consensus on the meaning of creativity, it is not surprising that ideas of how to foster this human capacity vary according to personal views. So it is more important to understand how creativity is interpreted by the teachers than to try to define it. It thus makes sense to discuss the approaches employed by practitioners in different social contexts to foster creativity from their own perspective and the teachers from the two kindergartens can offer us local knowledge about these approaches. Drawing on the examples of art work activities presented in Chapter 7, we look at the Chinese teachers' interpretations of creativity.

How teachers at Girassol interpret creativity

The teachers I first interviewed about their ideas of learning and the new pedagogies also participated in this set of interviews. Most had first heard of the term creativity in the 1990s when receiving in-service teacher training to upgrade their qualifications to University level. Thereafter, they read about creativity in journal articles and elsewhere. They used a variety of terms to describe what creativity means for them.

The meaning of creativity

The Girassol teachers both agree and disagree about what creativity means. The headteacher focuses on the different manifestations of creativity in its finished form. Vong *sin san*, on the other hand, asserts that creativity implies something unusual while Lo *sin san* draws on the similarity between the sense of beauty and creativity, in that both are difficult to grasp and to teach, and both involve her pupils' personal feelings. But despite these differences, three key similarities can be identified from the responses. First, all three teachers believe that creativity is the manifestation of personal thinking and feelings:

Headteacher Leong: *In art work, it is about an object. But it is not necessarily an object, it could be personal thinking ...*

Vong sin san: *not repressing what one has inside, ... using one's thinking to express something, creativity is something very personal*

Lo sin san: *something thought of, whatever she thinks it is, ... other people might not think so ... it is a personal feeling*

Second, they all suggest that creativity means thinking or making something new, with some kind of freedom:

Headteacher Leong: *... with given resources, and space, children can make a new thing which never existed before*

Vong sin san: *... something that one thinks of doing, not under restrictions*

Lo sin san: *Give them free rein*

Third, the headteacher and Vong *sin san* describe creativity as a natural human capacity which, depending on whether or not it is nurtured, may thrive or disappear:

Headteacher Leong: *Everyone has the potential to create ... if everything restricts it, it might withdraw gradually.*

Vong sin san: *Creativity is something born with ... if not fostered, creativity will disappear.*

To these practitioners, creativity is innate but needs to be nurtured in a non-restrictive social environment or it will not thrive.

Elements of creativity

Spradley (1979) has suggested that it is more useful to find out 'how' the participants apply their understanding of the term creativity in their everyday life and at work and not just ask 'what' questions. We can probe deeper by drawing on Smith's (1996) idea that asking 'funnelling' questions can reveal participants' deeper thoughts and conceptions. Accordingly, I invited the Girassol teachers to comment on what they conceive as the elements of creativity, and their ideas proved very different ideas.

The headteacher argues that basically, flexibility, elaboration, fluency and imagination are the core elements through which creativity will be manifested:

Headteacher Leong: *... through these elements, creativity is given free rein to manifest*

The elements she cites are the ones listed in the reference material for teachers on creativity published by the local education authority, but they are not mentioned by the two class teachers. Vong *sin san* is more concerned with the involvement of the individual in the activities. She suggests that willingness to take risks is an important element of creativity.

Vong sin san: *... dare to try out new ideas ..., not afraid of making mistakes, not worrying too much whether it resembles something or not*

She shares with Lo *sin san* the view that close observation which allows one to see the details of things is another key element. However, Lo *sin san* regards thinking through imitation and gaining recognition from other people as essential elements of creativity.

Lo sin san: *... everything is the result of thinking while imitating ... creativity needs other people's recognition, ... if not, you will be afraid to carry on with that*

Lo *sin san's* interpretation of creativity is thus a mix of ideas. She had said that 'creativity is about the sense of beauty ... it's about personal feelings' and here she is stating that it needs recognition by others. And her comments on the role of imitation support Vong *sin san's* view on the relationship between learning and imitation expressed earlier.

These diverse views are intriguing given that the three participants define creativity in notably similar ways. It seems that the headteacher is drawing on certain literature to talk about what makes something creative, as she uses the abstract constructs that appear in official printed matter, whereas the two teachers draw primarily on their own teaching experiences. Lo *sin san's* contrasting responses, in particular her emphasis on imitation, might imply that some Chinese teachers' understanding of creativity is embedded in indigenous Chinese educational ideas.

Approaches to fostering creativity

Do the three interviewees also differ over the approaches to foster creativity in children?

Both teachers focus on various subject areas such as music (singing, dancing, rhythmic activities), children's rhymes, group discussions led by teachers' questioning techniques, and art work (construction activities using junk materials, drawing) as the media through which they foster creativity in the children. In a subtle way, Vong *sin san* links the different possibilities that art work activities provide – working together, technical skills and drawing, etc – with the development of creativity.

Vong sin san: *... art work provides different domains, such as working together ... cooperation can be fostered, in the process, cutting, drawing are involved ... in a lesson, besides creativity, children have to learn other skills, creativity can be learned through art work, so is being part of a group and getting along with others.*

The role of artwork activities in fostering creativity is echoed by Lo *sin san*, who points out that in artwork there are no right or wrong answers. She suggests that creativity, like aesthetics, is about personal feelings, so cannot be taught; rather, teachers should inspire this feeling in children. The teachers' role in children's cognitive development is vital.

Lo sin san: *It's a personal feeling, so we have to inspire this generation's feeling for beauty.*

The Girassol teachers think it important to give children the space and freedom to think and make choices as often as possible.

Headteacher Leong: *... the potential to create exists in everyone, through different situations, different spaces or different thinking process, there comes different creativity ... if everything restricts her ... or there is only one answer for her, her creativity might fade away*

Vong sin san: *give her some freedom, give her some space for thinking*

The teachers emphasise the value of guided discussions with the children about the topic of interest.

Vong sin san: *... besides encouraging them, it is necessary to accept some opinions, meanwhile we give them some comments and information ... besides letting them do it, sin san have to give them some information on the side, an information which guides them to observe events and objects, whether correct or not, which is better, and let them choose*

Lo sin san: *... focus on questioning, foster their thinking and let them talk about their many answers*

These responses suggest that the Girassol teachers have integrated a more socially-oriented and child-centred approach into their previously teacher-centred one.

Emotional support, praise and encouragement are also considered necessary for promoting creativity. An episode that Vong *sin san* is proud of exemplifies the guidance and non-judgmental discourses used by the teachers to help children realise their weaknesses:

Vong sin san: *... Just like when we are about to open a new scotch tape, if we start by telling them that they did not tape the pieces together nicely, they will panic. We have to modify our language, we say, 'If you go shopping, will you ... will you buy something like that?' Then we will request them to do a better job when taping.*

Vong *sin san* maintains that teachers should not accept everything children do. Rather, they should help children, in an indirect and non-threatening manner, to see their mistakes so they can learn from them. Thus the social factors in fostering children's creativity and learning are emphasised.

Taken together, the Girassol teachers' approaches to fostering creativity are relatively open-ended. They depend on the teachers' role in guiding, accepting and supporting the ideas of children. They find that the nature and extent of space and freedom accorded the children ranges from asking them open-ended questions to think about, just giving them a theme to work around or some information as a basis for discussion before or during junk construction activities, to more teacher-directed activities such as teaching them some basic ideas in, say, music or language, and encouraging them to think of their own lyrics and movements. So the kind of 'frames', guidance or support can vary from teacher to teacher and from activity to activity. Besides, to be creative, children themselves have to be observant and able to make choices.

Customs teachers' interpretation of creativity

The mainland teachers were also interviewed to determine their understanding of creativity. At the time of the second interviews, the science teacher who was preparing for an inter-departmental transfer could afford time only to comment on the teaching approaches in the classrooms (see Chapter 6). Two months later she was transferred to another division of the Customs Department.

The meaning of creativity

I used the same questions in the interviews with the teachers in both schools. Most said they first heard of creativity only in the late 1980s or early 1990s while attending teacher training programmes at normal schools or after they were employed. Their ideas about creativity come mainly from books, journal articles and their headteacher. When they talk about the meaning of creativity, each has a different focus.

The headteacher emphasises the initiation of children into exploration, thought and manipulation of materials. Zhou *lao shi* suggests that children always employ new ways of thinking to solve problems and this to her is creativity. Zhang *lao shi* regards creativity as the manifestation of integrated knowledge and skills. Thus, children's ability to innovate demands different knowledge and skills. Zhong *lao shi*, who majored in art education during her teacher training, considers the main features of creativity to be changing of ideas and forms. To her, creativity requires having first to acquire foundational knowledge and skills before one can make changes in things and ideas. Ding *lao shi*, who had just graduated and become a kindergarten teacher, thinks that creativity is about a transformational process during which an individual brings forth new ideas out of the old. The three interest group teachers (art, dance and English) describe creativity as a process: it is based on what teachers explain in a lesson before giving the children free rein so that they can develop their own thinking. However, the results should meet certain requirements or reach a specific goal. Moreover, it seems that the interpretation of creativity has changed over time. Zhong *lao shi* relates her idea of creativity to working experiences:

> *My initial understanding of creativity was that it was something of one's free desire ... being away from normal reasoning was creativity, being in strange forms was creativity ... but after working for a long time, I feel*

that there must be a very strong skill in it ... and a solid foundation in it before you can let go your imagination and then tell others how you create this thing with theories and evidence ...

She goes on, however:

In the past, the feeling was, it was like children could ..., could follow teachers' way of thinking, and manipulate with their own hands or, say, extend some kind of thinking, could think, could do things that were somewhat different from the teachers' or there was some, some innovation. Now it's like ... the extent is much greater. Creativity is like ... the teachers' basic requirements, or say the extent of guidance, can be much smaller, and then children's creativeness and innovation should be much greater.

Both teachers have moved away from their initial understanding of creativity. Zhou *lao shi*'s current approach is to allow more room for children to take part in their learning whereas Zhong *lao shi* has learned from her teaching experiences that children need to be taught more knowledge and skills than she once thought. It appears that both teachers have experienced conceptual changes in their understanding of creativity as their teaching experiences escalate and more thought is given to it. These responses suggest that the meaning of creativity is pre-conceived and that is contingent upon change and on each individual's experiences, beliefs and psychological constructs of the term.

Even though creativity means something different to each participant, its key characteristics can be identified from their accounts. Zhou *lao shi,* for example, said: ... create and work with own hands while Zhang *loa shi* said: anything operational, manifest their feelings upon listening to a piece of music or constructing ... putting into action.

Most participants identified *originality* – but it appears in different forms:

Zhang lao shi: *It's an ability to innovate ... the process of absorbing knowledge and then accepting it, then apply to innovation.*

Zhong lao shi: *... to renew something, to change it, modify it based on its foundation*

Zhou lao shi: *... have new thinking or new ideas*

Most of the teachers interviewed share a view that creativity is an ability to apply new ideas which stem from the knowledge and skills they acquire from teachers. These are experienced kindergarten teachers who have been able to see the effects of their teaching on children's development. As well as emphasising skills training, the Customs teachers are concerned with whether or not children are given the foundation and building blocks to develop the kind of thinking, whatever it may be, required for creativity. Hence they see the teachers' role as crucial. When the teacher's directive role is strongly believed to be a critical part of children's development of creativity, the question arises of how much encouragement and room children are given to extend their ideas and thinking or, more generally, to exercise their active role as learners.

Elements of creativity

The mainland teachers stress certain elements of creativity, such as the refinement or extension of foundation knowledge and abilities. There is a strong suggestion that creativity is an extended activity or idea from what has already been learned. This point underscores the significant role of teachers in its development:

Art teacher: *... prior to every creation there must be an experience*

Dance teacher: *... having some knowledge about things or events*

English teacher: *... there should be something underneath creativity as its foundation*

Another element of creativity has to do with a person's observational and technical skills and their ability to realise their thinking with their hands. The teachers regard basic knowledge and the ability to manifest ideas or thinking through their hands as significant indicators of creativity, but highlight the role of adults in the process.

Zhou lao shi: *... fine observation ... operate with own hands*

117

Zhang lao shi:	*... observation ... ability to apply materials ... ability to apply knowledge ... ability to apply skills*
Art teacher:	*... teachers and parents provide certain conditions and make him actualise this creativity ... manifest by their hands or by other means*

Some participants regard abstract thinking as an element in creativity. Self-expression and the originality of ideas and what is produced are usually considered important. The implication is that it is adults and what they can do for children's learning that is crucial in children's development of creativity.

Zhou lao shi:	*... thinking is relatively open and wide*
Zhang lao shi:	*... thinking is relatively wide ... imagination*

Fostering creativity

Headteacher Chen would like to set guidelines and provide examples for the teaching approaches and strategies at her kindergarten. She is convinced that if creative education is the core of education for Chinese children, the key issue is to change the teachers' conceptions about teaching. She believes that only then can the teaching activities in the classrooms be changed. Thus she expects the teachers at Customs to see their role in the teaching and learning process from a new and unfamiliar perspective.

Headteacher Chen:	*At first, my requirement for teachers is very simple. In the past, you constrained them tightly, now you let go. In the past, you taught them a lot, now you teach less, ask more questions, children answer, and you do not tell them how to do it. In the past, you told them how to do, now you expect that they do things. You encourage them to explore. It's like teachers take on a different role, not doing everything for them, changing oneself to be a guiding figure, assuming the function of inspiring and guiding.*

How well are these requirements understood by her staff? The teachers emphasise their concern to stimulate children's imagination and thinking. They consider art work activities and music, which involve body movements, as essential. But their general comments on fostering creativity are abstract and it is unclear how they apply to the classroom. For instance,

> Zhong lao shi: *activate their thinking*
>
> Zhang lao shi: *foster imagination ... culture sense of aestheticism through music*

The teachers' accounts indicate that their strategies are primarily teacher-directed:

> Zhong lao shi: *... the teacher fosters their abilities, fosters their abilities and skills when they begin hands on activities*
>
> Art teacher: *I used the same painting to demonstrate two pupils' paintings that differ from and are similar to my painting – both have creativity. There's imagination, one child imagined that there is an empty pond, and the other imagined the beautiful posture of two lotuses.*

The teachers do more than providing children with one-way transmission of knowledge and skills through demonstration: they leave some leeway for the children's own role in developing creativity. The supplementary strategies they suggest fit with their interpretation of creativity. For instance:

> Zhou lao shi: *... the teacher gives children some [musical] segments and lets them design some movements, create some movements in music lessons*
>
> Ding lao shi: *... let children modify stories or continue with the [unfinished] stories [told by teachers]* (my brackets)

The teachers also describe how they use children's work and the children themselves as role models in their teaching. They value the social aspect of learning activities, as being an effective means to foster creativity in the children. But they do not encourage social interaction amongst the children during art work activities.

Thus the headteacher's requirements for fostering creativity and the expectations of the Customs teachers are based on the teachers taking on a role which allows more room for children to develop their abilities while they support the process. The teachers are aware of the headteacher's requirements and endeavour to realise them through their everyday teaching strategies. However, the art work activities observed reveal that their pedagogy is still predominantly teacher-directed, even when adapting to the Project Approach. Clearly, independent thinking or personal ideas are not a priority in their pedagogy.

Children's creativity – meanings and promotion
The teachers' responses to the open-ended questions regarding creativity suggest that their ideas of creativity are more complicated than the teaching strategies observed in the classrooms.

The meaning of creativity
The Girassol Kindergarten teachers, including headteacher Leung, believe that creativity is about personal thinking and feelings. It is an innate ability, best fostered in a non-restrictive social environment. In contrast, at Customs, the meaning of creativity is contingent upon change and each teacher's experiences. They generally associate with originality. To them creativity means an ability to apply acquired skills and knowledge to new situations, thereby highlighting the teachers' role in the emergence and development of creativity in children.

Constructs of the elements of creativity
The teachers at Girassol talk about flexibility, elaboration, fluency, imagination and the children's willingness to take risks, though they do also mention imitation and observation. They take the view that for something to be considered creative, it should earn the recognition of other people. This is a social aspect of creativity: striving for approval encourages children to act creatively.

The Customs teachers see creativity differently: as children being able to extend or refine the foundational knowledge and abilities they have been taught by teachers through imagination and the ability to realise their thinking. They too note that creativity has a social aspect – learning from certain models of behaviour. This emphasis on the social differs from the ideas held at Girassol Kindergarten in subtle ways.

How children's creativity can be fostered

The Girassol teachers assert that providing space and freedom for children to think and make choices in subjects such as music, physical movement and art work is their main strategy for creativity, and they ask guiding questions to inspire the children's thinking. Giving children emotional support is considered another effective strategy. The Customs teachers, except for headteacher Chen, generally believe that teachers should teach by means of direct demonstration so as to build up children's basic knowledge and skills before they are allowed to extend their ideas or thinking. Modelling can also be through classmates and their work.

The Girassol teachers' perspectives and ideas about fostering creativity are closer to the ideas advocated by Western scholars (see Chapter 3), while the Customs teachers' views and teaching methods have more in common with the educational ideas valued by Chinese scholars in mainland China. Since teachers at both kindergartens share the same Chinese culture, these differences are both interesting and perplexing. We might be able to understand them better if we examine their own schooling experiences and the paths they followed in their professional development.

9

The life histories of the teachers

Life history allows us to stand back and examine our own and other people's experiences of schooling, as data to be analysed, compared and interpreted, and can lead us to a more considered, better informed view which may reaffirm us in what we are doing or, alternatively, lead to change of some kind. (Goodson and Sikes, 2001:73)

Gardner (1989) called for a broad understanding of creativity and its relationship with education, individual biographies and culture. To further illumine the transformational process of the pedagogy for creativity, we examine the life histories of the Chinese practitioners. Their early experiences of schooling shed some light on education systems in China from the 1960s to 1990s. They describe their experiences of the pedagogical strategies practised during their years of schooling and over the course of their in-service professional development.

The educational biographies of the Girassol teachers

All the teachers interviewed at Girassol Kindergarten have more than ten years teaching experience and all intend to stay in the job for a long time. Here they discuss their schooling experiences.

On the curriculum they reported as follows:

Headteacher Leung: *My kindergarten was a school of nature ... there were a lot of fruit trees, ... every day, our snacks were made from the fruits on our campus ... there*

	was a large sand pit, a large garden, a large activity room and a large playground ... the school environment made a deep impression on me.
Vong sin san:	*My family immigrated from mainland China to Macao when I was 3 years old ... I entered kindergarten when I was already 7 years old, so they put me in the 6-year-old class. When I started kindergarten, the words that we had to write were very difficult, I remember writing the word tree (樹). It was an evening kindergarten ... there wasn't any music lesson or physical education, ... Chinese, English and mathematics were the main subjects, in art, there was some painting ...*
Lo sin san:	*My family was quite rich ... I entered a day kindergarten. We had birthday parties ... there were songs. Teachers would play music and we sang along, there was everything ...*

Thus the teachers had very different early experiences although they were of similar age. Their childhood memories reflect the variation in practice and curriculum of kindergartens in the Macao community at the time and confirm the account in Chapter 4 on the variety of schools in Macao. Headteacher Leung's memory of her kindergarten days illustrate that one's early experiences can have a profound impact on one's ideas about education. Impressed by gardening and related activities in her childhood experience, she has incorporated gardening activities in Girassol.

Pedagogy was 'traditional'. All three teachers describe their foundation education in these terms:

Vong sin san:	*Traditional, each person sits in one seat ...*
Lo sin san:	*Traditional means, teacher talks, and students have to accept all.*

Their version of a traditional Chinese pedagogy includes certain features:

■ the disciplines are independent of one another

124

- teachers deliver lessons and children sit in rows and listen to what the teachers have to say

- there is no discussion between teacher and pupils or amongst the pupils

- almost all teachers expect children to recite after them or copy what they had done, for example in drawing, music and Chinese literature. Opportunities for children to decide what to do or how to do something did not arise.

As the headteacher summed up:

Headteacher Leong: What we call traditional is that the teacher will teach you, if it's a word, teach you that word, if it's a song, teach you that song, meaning, ... e ... will not give you space for thinking, only passing on knowledge to you.

They reported that at the time of their foundation schooling, almost all schools in the Macao community practised traditional education and described the teachers' pedagogical approaches as strongly teacher-centred. Those who encouraged discussions with students were rare.

Headteacher Leong: If we talk about art at kindergarten, there were a lot of tearing and pasting tasks. If there was a picture of a triangle, then you tore it out of the page and pasted it on the outline of a triangle ... when I was in secondary school, there was one teacher, who was good, that was Chinese composition class. The teacher would discuss the content with us after marking ...

Teacher education

These teachers' experiences of traditional education and a teacher-centred approach extended into their initial teacher training – which was offered as an evening programme by a local secondary school. Professional skills like teaching methods were taught and professional knowledge such as moral education, general education and psychology.

Vong sin san: *Even in the initial teacher training [an evening programme for pre-service teachers] school, it was like that, the teacher drew a picture, and you follow. ... maybe, in the era, had not developed ideas of ... creative thinking, I think ... But at least the skills taught and learned were useful when we entered a kindergarten classroom. How would I know otherwise? But they did not require us to develop from there ... Subjects included moral education, general education, psychology, and different teaching methods ...*

Lo sin san: *... it was all like that, the teacher said something, the students accepted all on the list. Students were not asked to comment on things ... even for art, it was like that.*

It is clear that the kind of pedagogy employed by most teachers in Macao before the 1990s, from kindergarten to higher education, emphasised the teachers' role rather than learners' in the teaching and learning process.

Upgrading qualifications and changing educational ideas

As the Girassol teachers had obtained their teacher qualification some 10 to 15 years ago, they were required to upgrade their knowledge and skills periodically. During the upgrading – phase one – they were gradually exposed to more liberal pedagogical approaches at the faculty of education of a local university. Staff at the faculty are mostly educated in Western countries such as Germany, England, America, Australia, Canada and Belgium so will have encountered ideas of Western educational pedagogies. The practitioners had mixed experience during the upgrading, from teacher-centred pedagogy to educational ideas that were new to them, for instance about creative thinking.

Headteacher: *During this learning experience, um ... I came to know about ideas of creative thinking, or about visual arts, I feel that in these respects, in fact, there is a lot of space for children ...*

126

Vong sin san:　　　*During the first upgrading, if we talk about art, it was pretty much the same. Given a picture, you copy it. There was no music lesson. But the lesson plans looked different, meaning, it was much clearer. The format was different ...*

A few years later they returned to the same university for the second phase of upgrading their qualifications.

Lo sin san:　　　*During phase one, we learned how to organise groups of children to work on different tasks, it was chaotic at the beginning. During phase two of our qualification upgrading, it was one year, we learned how to create learning centres and organise children to use these centres in the classroom. Before that, I did not know how to handle lessons involving learning centres ...*

During phase two, the pedagogies and ideas of kindergarten education were moving towards a child-centred approach which gives children more room and freedom to interact with their learning environment.

The ideas were influenced by eminent Western early childhood educators. One of the class teachers said:

Vong sin san:　　　*I remember Rousseau. I feel that, the way he sees children, in fact, human beings are a natural kind of thing, so they will take on things that are given to them naturally ... and also Dewey, I have heard of his name, he advocated that something like education is in everyday life ... In fact, these theories are similar in meaning ... ie do not strive sedulously on learning, make them sit still, should let them learn unknowingly.*

Western educational ideas were bound to affect their views of education and teaching approaches. Being teachers at public kindergartens, their pedagogy has also been influenced by the in-service training plans designed for them by the local education department.

Vong sin san: *The latest upgrading should be relatively better as it is following the trend of kindergarten education. Things are changing and changing all the time, in fact, the first year of initial teacher training and the last year of training at the faculty of education are most useful ...*

Lo sin san: *I also think that the one year, ie phase two teacher training is most useful ...*

Governmental in-service teacher development plans

All *Luso-Chinês* kindergarten teachers have to attend different seminars as part of their professional development. Since the Macao SAR government began promoting the idea of teaching for creative thinking, the local Education and Youth Bureau has organised seminars, conferences and workshops on this topic. Taiwanese scholars, themselves educated in America, have been invited to Macao SAR to share their ideas on ways to foster creativity in children. The Bureau often organises study trips to Taiwan, mainland China, Hong Kong SAR, Singapore and New Zealand, for example, so that teachers at *Luso-Chinês* Schools can learn with their counterparts.

To sum up, the Girassol teachers' educational background shows that throughout their professional training, their ideas of early childhood education and children's learning have been steadily influenced by Western educational ideas and a learner-centred approach.

The educational biographies of Customs teachers

The headteacher and class teachers at Customs Kindergarten were invited to reveal their life history. This time, the science teacher was back for the interview. The teachers were mostly born in the early 1980s and many graduated from Normal Schools in the late 1990s. Like the headteacher, who was born in the 1960s, almost all are from parts of mainland China, such as the Guangxi Zhuang Autonomous Region in the west, Hunan Province in the south, the central Anhui Province, Liaoling Province and Heilongjiang Province in the north. This makes their life histories more varied and intriguing.

Early experiences of schooling
1) Curriculum

Headteacher Chen: *Well, I finished my foundational education in Guangxi, from Kindergarten to Secondary School, ..., in my impression, there were activities, story telling, playing with toys, games, and then meals, and then went home for a nap after lunch ..., it was a happy childhood ... I remember listening to the story Little Red Hat, it was during the time of cultural revolution, I asked myself, would it be an activists' story ...*

Science teacher: *I actually went through kindergarten education ... The teachers were all middle-aged women, it was mainly care-taking ... I remember at that time, in 1975 or 76, chairman Mao died ... there were several dozen children at the kindergarten ... all were gathered in the courtyard, facing the main door ... teacher gave signal, all had to lower our heads.*

Zhong lao shi: *When I was young ... I was raised in an indulged manner, not taught by established practice ... My mom was a member of the art troupe, and then I learned dancing, art, poems ... the direction was leading to arts ... after all, my mom did not care about my academic performance ... so my kindergarten and primary school education was wasted under these circumstances ...*

These accounts drew a picture of the political atmosphere in mainland China which influenced even very young children. During their childhood, kindergarten programmes were apparently not academically oriented. Some kindergartens focused on activities such as story time, playing with toys and games, while others employed untrained adults to provide nothing more than care-taking services. These are examples of only some of the teachers' early experiences. Others did not reveal their life story as fully but the following information was extracted from the collected accounts.

2) Pedagogy

The teachers interviewed at Customs Kindergarten came to Zhuhai SER from various parts of mainland China. They differ in age and the kinds of schools they attended. Are their experiences of pedagogy and pedagogical approaches similar?

> *Headteacher Chen:* *During my time ... kindergarten education was not formal at all, there were only games, toys, meals, stories. There wasn't anything to teach, or learn ... When we entered primary school, we had some formal teaching and learning ... I feel that that kind of pedagogy was rather traditional, that is, to inculcate knowledge, that was fairly common ... that means to let you read books, let you write words, read to you and you wrote down, read aloud the chapters. There was little use of inspiring methods, or let children discuss, interact, very seldom, meaning the teacher lectured, and you listened ... Even in secondary school, it was more or less like that ... Even in Quangxi Normal School for Early Childhood Education, it was the same, from 1980 to 82 ...*

The kind of traditional pedagogy headteacher Chen experienced continued well into early adulthood. Even though her interpretation of learning, cognition and creativity resonate with Western interpretations, she feels that kindergarten education should not be just about toys, meals, stories, and games, but that there should also be something to teach and learn.

> *Science teacher:* *At my kindergarten, ... Teaching was done orally, one time not enough, twice, doing this repeatedly until we memorised it ... that was in 1973, 74 ... In primary school, teaching was like stuffing ducks, very stern, just to inculcate knowledge, ... In terms of arts, ... in drawing, the teacher drew one picture first, then students drew one, just imitation, ... In secondary school, there were more subjects, ... there was no interaction between teacher and*

> *students, it was very boring. The teacher just*
> *talked on the podium, read out the chapter ...*

The science teacher offers a detailed account of her early experiences of Chinese education and pedagogy. This was essentially a one-way transmission model, teacher-centred, where learning occurred by means of pre-designed activities where teachers demonstrated and children imitated.

Experiences in teacher education

The class teachers, Zhong *lao shi* and Ding *lao shi* paired up for an interview session. Each had a slightly different background. Zhong *lao shi* was an art major at the normal school and graduated in the mid 1990s. Ding *lao shi* got her teacher qualification in 1999 but continued to study for a higher qualification directly after finishing the initial three years of teacher training.

Zhong lao shi: *At normal school, I feel that the teachers could not leave the podium, leave the blackboard, it's like ... the teaching method was no different from the previous stages of my schooling ... eg in sewing, that's to teach, first told you about the contours, that's to make the paper sample of these clothes, demonstrated on the paper, after demonstrating, asked someone to be the model and cut the piece of cloth ...*

Ding lao shi: *It was teacher-centred, in Heilongjiang ... in art, the main teaching method was to demonstrate first and then we put hands on ... there was a drawing book, the teacher 'moved' the picture to the board, and we 'moved' it to our sketch book ... I feel that during the last two years of my teacher training education, ... basically they don't teach you much. During the three years, the teachers would still teach you something, but then they basically don't teach much anymore ...*

Ding *lao shi*'s account revealed that by the late 1990s the pedagogy employed by teachers at Normal Schools was changing, requiring students to play a more active role in their learning.

Another two class teachers interviewed together had similar pedagogical experiences. They reported that uniform teaching materials were strictly followed by teachers across China. The main focus of their Normal Schools was to establish teacher-trainees' skills and techniques.

Zhou lao shi: *... I feel that before, there should be, that is, a set of uniform teaching materials – eh – a uniform teaching material, then what was taught and learned was basically the content of the materials ... In normal school, from 1987 to 90, our school fostered our skills and techniques, personal skills and techniques, skills and techniques are dancing, singing, piano, handicrafts, drawing, these subjects ... teaching methods ... the teacher would give me a model, how to teach, how to ... it's like in mathematics, how to teach 'one and many', the teacher would tell you fully ... how to do it, but the teaching methods were similar to those in primary and secondary schools ....*

Zhang lao shi: *... the teacher would tell you these techniques, that is – eh – colouring, putting the pen on paper, designing, how to, what should be done, which things to pay attention to, and then demonstrate ... then we practise for half of the lesson time.*

Zhou *lao shi* and Zhang *lao shi*'s narratives of their early experiences of Chinese education share many similarities with their counterparts from different parts of mainland China.

Upgrading qualifications and critical changes in educational ideas
Some Customs teachers take up in-service teacher education to upgrade their qualifications. This kind of higher education is characterised by lectures and seminars and the approach tends to be less directive. Despite these experiences of schooling, the teachers said their ideas of education had changed.

Headteacher Chen: *The critical changes in my educational ideas took place when I was assigned as a researcher to the*

> *Nannin Research Institute in Quangxi after my*
> *graduation from teachers' normal school. I was*
> *there for eight years as a researcher ... I read a lot of*
> *books or theories, and I paid close attention to the*
> *educational reforms abroad and inside China ... I*
> *had to attend conferences, research activities, etc...*

As a researcher, headteacher Chen had had opportunities to study educational ideas and pedagogical approaches practised in different countries. She studied Western and Chinese theories and exchanged ideas with Western and Chinese scholars and this has strongly influenced her current ideas.

Work experiences can change teachers' educational ideas because it allows them to put theories and skills to the test, learn from their headteachers and test their abilities.

> *Science teacher:* *I feel that what we learned at Normal School was*
> *a foundation ... including ideas of education and*
> *teaching methods of various subjects, ... but the*
> *biggest influence came from headteacher Chen ...*
> *She's brought new ideas into the kindergarten ...*

> *Zhong lao shi:* *One was the tasks delegated by our leaders, then*
> *let you finish something all by yourself ... because*
> *in the entire process she lets us think, to make*
> *things somehow different from others', how to*
> *make something which would be recognised by*
> *everyone, I feel that's already ...*

All these mainland Chinese teachers at Customs Kindergarten were certainly trained according to the traditional Chinese pedagogy. Except for the headteacher, who reports coming across the theories of some renowned early childhood educators (Froebel, Dewey, Bloom, Rousseau, Piaget and Montessori), most of the teachers cannot recall any theories they learned. The fact that no educational theory has impressed them might imply that the pedagogies they employ today are primarily informed by their experience as students and at work. As Zhong *lao shi* explained,

... the main thing is that that is not the focus of teacher training educa-tion, so what we've learned ... are the skills and techniques

Governmental in-service teacher development plans

Since the National Education Bureau is calling for reform and en-couraging teachers to foster creativity in children, there could be many ways to update the teachers at Customs Kindergarten on the latest ap-proaches, home-grown or advocated by foreign countries, which might lead to more discussion and thinking about pedagogy. The Zhuhai Edu-cational Bureau is obliged to inform, organise or notify kindergarten teachers about the availability of documents, seminars and workshops on creativity or creative education. However, for various reasons, most kindergartens only subsidise a few teachers to take part in professional development opportunities in mainland China. This means that infor-mation is filtered and interpreted by many others before it reaches individual teachers. And these teachers have relatively few oppor-tunities to visit overseas educational settings. In short, their primary source of information on creative education and related pedagogies comes from articles and books authored by Chinese educators.

Teachers' life histories and professional practice

The three teachers at Girassol Kindergarten in Macao SAR share similar educational backgrounds and experiences despite their different social and economic backgrounds. As Goodson and Sikes (2001) suggested, 'Professional work cannot and should not be divorced from the lives of professionals' (p71). Although the kind of pedagogy the three teachers experienced has gradually moved from a traditional teacher-centred approach to a learner-centred one, their early educational experiences can still strongly influence their current ideas about teaching and learn-ing. The construction activities and the practitioners' ideas of learning and cognition presented in Chapter 6 illustrate the influence of in-digenous educational ideas. They take the view that imitation does not prevent creativity or independent thinking. Conceptual changes are not that easy, especially when non-indigenous ideas such as creativity are being transplanted from a different culture. Even so, increasing ex-posure to Western theories and practice has influenced these teachers' educational ideas and pedagogical strategies.

On the other side of the Gate, we see some flexibility and variation in teaching styles, even though most of the teachers at Customs have been educated under the Chinese traditional education system where pupils are not encouraged to develop their own thinking and ideas. The pedagogy employed by these teacher-trainers is likely to influence their own ideas and classroom pedagogy. As we saw from the art work activities presented in Chapter 6, the mainland teachers' interpretations of learning, cognition and creativity are heavily influenced by the indigenous Chinese education system and this connects with their own educational biographies.

So that while the Girassol teachers' ideas and pedagogical approaches are still laden with Chinese traditional approaches, they are also substantially influenced by Western theory and pedagogical strategies. Quite the opposite is found amongst the mainland teachers, whose ideas are primarily based on Chinese traditional education. All the practitioners' life histories showed evidence that their early experiences affect how they teach now.

Each of the kindergartens has sought a creative programme and pedagogy in order to foster creativity in children. Embedded in the different social and economical contexts, school cultures and life histories, the pedagogical approaches developed appear to be rather culture-specific. The complexities of the transformational process to a new pedagogy are analysed next.

10

Creating a cultural product

Certain cultural themes can be identified that explain what I observed in each of the kindergartens. First, the kindergartens are culturally constructed, embedded in different social and cultural contexts. Secondly, children's cognitive development is a product of the participating teachers' interpretation of learning and cognition. Lastly, a creative pedagogical approach is culturally constructed in light of the social and economic contexts, school cultures and the Chinese practitioners' understanding of creativity.

Theme I – The expectations of the government and culturally constructed kindergartens

Two official documents that appeared at the beginning of the millennium provide direction for the educational settings in both mainland China and Macao SAR to encourage and develop children's creativity. This educational goal had received little attention until now, but it is being implemented in ways which will highlight the current position and the issues to be addressed. Stemming from the different social contexts under which the two kindergartens are operating, two kinds of schools have evolved.

Girassol Kindergarten – a mix of cultures and practices

As described earlier, Girassol Kindergarten reflects the *Luso-Chinês* that goes back several generations. Although the city of Macao is now under Chinese sovereignty, Western influence and particularly Portuguese culture are part of life and affect growth and development.

Macao originally established a liberal Portuguese curriculum and pedagogy designed for Portuguese children, based on learning through play. But many of the teachers are local Chinese. As the political situation changes, the curriculum and pedagogy of the schools have been modified by Chinese teachers to cater for Chinese children but signs of Portuguese educational ideas are still noticeable. The curriculum, pedagogical approach and physical environment of Girassol Kindergarten are a mixture of Chinese and Portuguese practices. There are two distinct features: the teachers are given leeway to develop their own character and they are greatly involved in the planning, implementation and reflective process of their new pedagogy.

Not only is the Kindergarten a product of *Luso-Chinês* culture, but the three teachers were either born in Macao or settled there at a very young age, so have lived and received their own education within the same culture. Their Chinese origin and experiences of Chinese traditional education have influenced their pedagogical ideas but their efforts to keep up with the trend in kindergarten education have exposed them to progressive pedagogical ideas and liberal approaches that are rooted in Western culture. The historical factors, school culture and teachers' life histories have all contributed to the unique character of Girassol Kindergarten – one that is embedded in a mix of Chinese and European influences and a team of teachers who are relatively well informed about various pedagogical approaches and open to different educational ideas.

Customs Kindergarten – a product of the Chinese social system

Zhuhai city has always been part of mainland China. Before the Open Door Policy was announced in 1979, few mainland Chinese had contact with the rest of the world. So there was little change in the educational arena. Although China has had more academic exchanges with their overseas counterparts over the past 20 to 30 years, along with its economic growth, these generally involve high ranking officials. Information is passed down from the national to the provincial, to the municipal level and then from the local education bureau to kindergartens, to headteachers and lastly to teachers. Thus the slippage between principles and practice easily occurs and is often overlooked. This hierarchical system continues at the school level.

Since Customs Kindergarten is under the authority of the Customs Department of Zhuhai SER, the curriculum, practice and pedagogical approaches are monitored by parents who are mostly Customs officers. This creates a hierarchical atmosphere in the school. The physical environment, curriculum and ways of discipline are all organised to facilitate the physical growth and moral development of children according to the priorities set by its superiors. Children are expected to learn from their teachers or more capable peers through modelling their deeds and ideas during formal lessons and informal activity time. Although teachers are aware that children should be respected as individuals, their pedagogical approach is primarily teacher-centred. Direct instructions are expected, imitation by other pupils is accepted and demonstration in teaching is prioritised over children's expression of ideas and thinking.

The mainland teachers' life histories are characterised by a traditional Chinese education. Their initial teacher training focused on building up their own skills and techniques (playing the piano, drawing, dancing, handicrafts, etc) rather than strengthening their theoretical background and examining various pedagogical approaches. Only the younger teachers who studied in the late 1990s experienced a more student-oriented pedagogy, possibly influenced by the call for educational reform to liberate students at all levels from traditional education. Teachers' knowledge about different educational ideas, including creativity and modern trends, has been acquired from their headteacher and from educational journals published in mainland China. So they have no first hand knowledge about progressive educational practice.

All these factors have strongly influenced the character of Customs Kindergarten. Regimented within a monocultural context it offers an indigenous programme catering for the offspring of government officials. It has a team of teachers who are well trained in the techniques and skills endorsed by the Chinese educational and social system.

Theme II – Children's cognitive development as a product of teachers' interpretations of learning and cognition

According to the Piagetian or constructivist view of learning, children acquire knowledge and advance cognitively by interacting with the physical and material environment as their innate abilities mature. The Vygotskian or socio-cultural view advocates that children develop cognitively via social interactions with other people. Researchers who follow Vygotskian theorists, such as Wertsch, Rogoff, Lave, Hedegaard, Childs and Greenfield, Brown and Ferrara, provide evidence in school and other contexts that children acquire knowledge through interacting with more capable individuals who support and guide the learning processes. Cole (1985) suggested that culture and cognition are linked, and that they should not be considered independently. The evidence in my study, grounded in two different social contexts, supports Cole's theory and the socio-cultural theorists' view of children's learning and cognitive development. In particular, the role of demonstration and imitation in the teachers' pedagogy at both kindergartens and the role of teachers in children's learning deserve further discussion. The different approaches foster different abilities in the children. They are indeed the ways in which culture and cognition create each other.

Demonstration and imitation – a cultural and social practice

According to the practitioners' interpretation of children's learning and cognition at both kindergartens, especially Customs, demonstration and imitation are necessary for children's learning and cognitive development. Evidence was found in both kindergartens: (a) Chinese educational goals and pedagogy; (b) the teachers' transformed ideas about learning.

Chinese educational goals and pedagogy
Girassol Kindergarten

We saw in Chapter 4 how children at *Luso-Chinês* kindergartens are required to develop the skills required for mastering writing and other paper and pencil tasks. These tasks require strong visual memory, sharp observation, attention to detail and following the correct sequence of the strokes of Chinese characters, as well as hands-on abilities and fine motor skills. Teachers' demonstrations and children practising by imitation are crucial to the mastery of such skills. Moreover, children are traditionally regarded in Chinese culture as naive creatures who need to be nurtured by adults whom they should regard as role models. This is why demonstration and imitation is the dominant strategy for children's learning.

The Girassol Kindergarten teachers' discourses on the classroom activities described earlier reveal that the teachers regard imitation as a natural way children learn at this age, ie children acquire knowledge and abilities by imitating other people's work and behaviour. What is interesting is that all the teachers in my study are aware that these ideas have been passed down for generations. The teachers' life histories reveal that they experienced this kind of pedagogy during their own schooling so that Chinese ideas of learning still have currency. The children at Girassol Kindergarten also regard imitation as a kind of learning, but from friends rather than adults. I observed this during my fieldwork:

> ...They sat next to each other and both coloured the white drawing paper with bright yellow. When it was time to clean up, one of the girls added a strip of pink self-adhesive paper to the drawing and drew a few circles on it. Her friend saw that and quickly added a few circles to her own drawing. I asked this friend why she had added the circles to her drawing when they were putting their drawings away. She whispered to me, 'I learn it from her'. (Journal, 25 April, 2002)

Interestingly, the little girl who imitated her friend's idea answered my question by using the word 'learn' instead of 'copy' or 'imitate'. It seems that imitating what other people have done is considered in this social context as a means of learning.

Customs Kindergarten
Children at Customs are also required to learn writing and master paper and pencil tasks. Language abilities are important, especially the ability to read and the need to master a large volume of Chinese idioms, vocabulary, antonyms, rhymes and poems. All these are learned by following the adults orally and repeating what they say. Then there is an emphasis on craftsmanship, especially the mastery of traditional handicrafts such as paper folding and paper cutting. All these require the children to

have hands-on or technical skills, sharp observation and good memory and to receive demonstrations and explicit instructions from others.

The role played by demonstration and imitation is highlighted by Customs teachers' interpretation of learning. According to some of these teachers, children can learn from observing what others – both adults and peers – do. Both old and new meanings of learning pertain. The old is signified by adults showing, children imitating and the emphasis on the results of any learning activity rather than its process. The new concept advocates that learning is about independent thinking, personal experiences, initiative, creativeness, autonomy. Emphasis is on the process. Nonetheless, the predominant opinion considers that when children follow what others do (because they do not know) and then practise by themselves (ie progress to knowing), that is learning.

This understanding of learning is similar to that noted at Girassol Kindergarten but here the role of demonstration and imitation is given higher status and greater value. At Customs, the children seem to be engaged in this learning process all the time – during formal lessons, free drawing time, artwork activities, and especially when they are sitting together. Imitation can also be a sign of friendship.

> *These two girls are sitting next to each other and chatting to each other while drawing on their sketch book during free drawing time. Both drew a scene where children are eating at McDonald's. I asked them why they drew the 'same' picture. One of the girls said, 'She and I are good friends'. (Journal, 12 March, 2002)*

There is also evidence that whether one is imitating another's work or being imitated by others, the term 'learn' can be used to stand for 'imitate'.

> *The teacher told them to divide the drawing paper into different sections so as to indicate the different varieties of food observed during their field trip to the market that morning. Two children sitting next to each other both divided the rectangular drawing paper into four sections by drawing two lines perpendicular to each other in the centre of the page. I asked the one who first finished drawing the lines, 'Why does she divide the page into four parts in this way?' The girl replied, 'She learns it from me' and continued with her drawing. (Journal, 17 May, 2002)*

Obviously the teachers at both kindergartens were themselves educated by means of the demonstration and imitation. In short, all the observed phenomena at both kindergartens show that imitation is a natural and useful way for children to acquire information. And when imitation means learning, friendship and exchange of ideas to young Chinese, it is likely to persist in Chinese education in the future.

Teachers' transformed ideas about learning
Girassol Kindergarten
Not only do the teachers at Girassol believe that demonstration is sometimes necessary, some believe that while they are imitating, the children are also actively thinking. And children will note what they see others do, be inspired and then extend those ideas, along with their personal experiences and observations, to form their own ideas. More importantly, children are encouraged to extend the teachers' ideas and thinking. Thus, imitation is a product of communication with others as well as a means for children to advance cognitively. When adult and child or child and child converse about something, a matter for thinking about has been provided and that will lead to further thinking and learning. Setting the children the task of working out how they could make their air conditioner more realistic is a good example of the teacher trying to stimulate children's cognitive processes. It is significant that it is the teacher who is encouraging the children to extend their ideas. As one teacher remarked, 'learning is not about children learning on their own'.

The Girassol teachers are also aware of other possibilities for learning – by asking questions and taking risks in order to advance technically and cognitively. In traditional education, children are supposed to listen to and follow their teachers' ideas and are not expected to ask questions and test their new ideas as alternative means of learning. This is not part of the traditional pedagogy but is advocated by individualistic Western cultures (Gardner, 1989). Girassol Kindergarten teachers' views of learning share some similarities with what Gardner observed of the demonstration-imitation learning processes in mainland China about fifteen years ago, indicating that the Chinese idea of learning is essentially continued throughout Chinese culture. Gardner visited mainland China three times in the 1980s and his visits led him to assert that

143

imitation, although believed by scholars in the West to thwart creativity, did not necessarily harm its development. He maintained that 'one cannot begin to unravel issues of creativity and education without taking into account one's own reactions and system of values' (Gardner, 1989:15). My interviews reveal that the educational ideas of learning held by Girassol teachers have been broadened to take into account some Western educational ideas to which they might have been exposed during their professional development opportunities. But there is more to be said about learning.

The Girassol teachers' interpretation of learning and cognition which stress children's learning by imitation determines the main role of Chinese teachers, ie to provide modelling for children. They recognise that children's learning should be supported by the teachers' continuous guidance. Their approach involves much discussion between teachers and pupils and each learning activity is scaffolded throughout, whereas Customs teachers rely on providing direct answers and demonstrations.

The Girassol teachers' ideas of learning are in line with those of Chinese scholars who insist that teachers should assume the guiding position in the teaching and learning process (Pan, 1993) and should play a key role in inducing children to learn (Chen, 1996). However, they also reckon that children need social interaction with their peers, and room to develop their ideas and thinking in a non-restrictive learning environment. So the teachers empower children to learn by providing opportunities and conditions for them to work on their tasks while they play the role of facilitators. The guiding role they assume is informed by their ideas of learning and cognitive development – and these comprise both indigenous and foreign theories.

Customs Kindergarten

Some teachers at Customs believe that children have to imitate the work and ideas of others so as to learn the basic way to handle a task before they develop their own ideas and thinking. Imitation is considered not merely as straight copying but as a foundational step in the process of learning. This is exemplified by the art work activities in which the teachers encouraged children to add designs to a pen holder when the basics had been done according to a model, thus making sure that children acquire the foundational skills first. But the mainland teachers hold different opinions about imitation.

It appears that some of the teachers at Customs have conceptually different ideas of learning from the practitioners observed in earlier studies (Kessen, 1975; Tobin et al, 1989; Gardner, 1989) in mainland China. The notion of avoiding demonstration and imitation and instead emphasising individual thinking, like the notion of retrieving information and constructing knowledge from one's physical environment on one's own are not indigenous. The disparate interpretations of learning expressed in the interviews indicate that some Chinese teachers have been influenced by foreign understandings of learning and cognition. In this study, the Customs teachers appear to take different positions. The traditional ideas of learning are being challenged by 'new' concepts. The majority of the teachers at Customs still support the view that imitation is a foundational step to further learning, thus highlighting the specific characteristics of Chinese pedagogy.

The teaching of Customs staff is also informed by their interpretation of learning and cognition which highlights the teachers' belief in demonstration and instruction. However, when asked to comment on their pedagogical approach and that of the Girassol Kindergarten, these teachers only recognise certain ways in which teachers influence children's learning, such as by means of demonstrations, requiring them to finish tasks, and supporting children's learning with praise. But they do not realise the Girassol teachers' supportive role in scaffolding and guided participation in such a way that the responsibilities of the task are gradually shifted to the children. The teachers have to negotiate their pupils' ideas so they fit their ideas of how to work on a task. But the Customs teachers have apparently not developed the other roles that teachers can take on.

In sum, demonstration and imitation are still the dominant pedagogy in Chinese education. Imitation has been assigned a different meaning: it is considered not as mere copying but as a platform provided by teachers for children to make cognitive leaps. What the kindergartens share is the valuing of social interaction between children and adults. They display a socio-cultural perspective of learning which suggests that interaction amongst participants in social activities leads to the acquisition of knowledge.

Different approaches, different abilities

The teachers' perception of their role and the children's in learning determine their specific pedagogical approaches and thus stimulate different abilities in children. The Girassol teachers describe their pedagogy as open-ended, since the children are given free rein to think, work with ideas and materials and explore through personal experiences, in contrast to the pedagogy at Customs. They reckon that their approach provides children with basic technical skills such as how to hold scissors or apply scotch tape, but that it also fosters social skills such as collaborating with peers, communicating with teachers and peers, language skills when being critical, and abstract thinking – which embraces reflective thinking and creative thinking. The Girassol teachers believe that the Customs' approach can foster only technical skills and some knowledge about the object being made.

The teachers' ideas of learning at Girassol have embraced indigenous ideas of teaching and learning which value the teacher's guiding role and the children's responsibilities in making an effort to observe and imitate. We see a substantial infusion of Western educational ideas, such as respect for children's expression of ideas, feelings and imagination. Emphasis is placed on the children's interest in the learning process and enjoyment of the space and leeway the teachers give them to develop. Diagram A illustrates the form of fusion of Western and indigenous pedagogies observed at Girassol Kindergarten. And the children might be given even more space to develop in future, as a more open-ended pedagogical approach is desired. The contrast with Customs Kindergarten (Diagram B) is evident.

Despite their awareness of modern ideas about what learning means, the Customs teachers' pedagogy is more consistent with the 'old' meaning of learning. While there is some Western pedagogic influence, children are given little space to develop independent thinking and autonomy and the pedagogy is essentially teacher-centred. This phenomenon is noticed by the Customs teachers. They regard their own pedagogical approach as restrictive, dominated by teachers' demonstrations and children's imitation and limiting children's thinking. They acknowledge that the approach adopted by Girassol Kindergarten gives children space and time to work with materials autonomously and think independently; it also encourages their imagination and creative think-

Diagram A

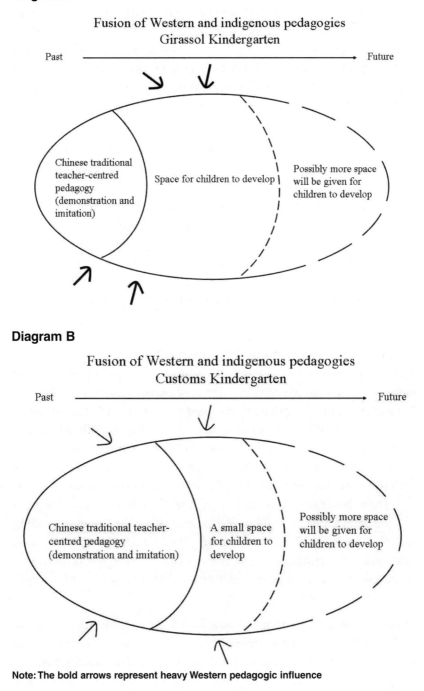

Fusion of Western and indigenous pedagogies
Girassol Kindergarten

Past ⟶ Future

Chinese traditional teacher-centred pedagogy (demonstration and imitation)

Space for children to develop

Possibly more space will be given for children to develop

Diagram B

Fusion of Western and indigenous pedagogies
Customs Kindergarten

Past ⟶ Future

Chinese traditional teacher-centred pedagogy (demonstration and imitation)

A small space for children to develop

Possibly more space will be given for children to develop

Note: The bold arrows represent heavy Western pedagogic influence

ing. The Customs teachers associate their approach with developing abilities such as technical skills and basic knowledge, and acknowledge that the approach at Girassol can foster the children's integrated abilities – simultaneously fostering basic technical skills plus creativeness and imagination. However, Customs may yet move towards a pedagogy which will allow children more room to develop independent thinking and autonomy, now that the advantages of a more child-centred approach are recognised.

It seems that when teachers provide a range of experiences for their children, giving them room to think and work with ideas and materials, the children can acquire a broader range of abilities, whereas teaching by giving children direct answers or demonstrations will limit their development almost entirely to basic technical skills. Cox *et al* (1999: 178) maintained that 'the differences in teaching might not have a significant effect on the level of the children's performance'. But this study shows that the different pedagogical approaches lead to differences in the scope of children's abilities and the kinds of thinking involved in an art work activity.

Culture and cognition creating each other

Tobin *et al* (1989) described how the Chinese culture and educational ideology in Taiwan, which was influenced by Japanese culture for over 50 years, remains essentially unchanged – a testament to the resilience of the Chinese culture. A bounce-back effect exists in both social contexts in my study: pedagogy is highly regulated because the teachers do not recognise what the children are gaining from the new pedagogy with its liberal nature in terms of learning and development of creativity. There is general concern amongst teachers that children should acquire solid foundational knowledge and skills. Yet Piaget, according to Cole, was concerned lest children made superficial rather than fundamental cognitive changes when adults tried to teach them in a context of imbalanced power relations and inattention to their cognitive levels (Cole, 1996).

But the Chinese teachers are coming from a different perspective. First, under traditional Chinese ideas of education, the results are as important as, if not more important than, the process of an activity. Second, the adults' role in caring and educating the naive and young still dominates the Chinese teachers' mentality. Third, teachers believe that they need to give a starting point for children's thinking – though the extent of this varies – or provide a direction for their ideas, and children will then take off to develop their ideas and thinking in different directions.

The advantages of imitation in children's learning have in fact been supported by some studies in mainland China (Cox *et al*, 1999; Winner, 1989). Although teachers have learned about Western pedagogies, the essence of Chinese traditional pedagogy, namely the teacher's role – which may vary – in children's learning has thrived in Chinese contexts to this day. There is evidence that in both social contexts children's cognitive development is a product of the different forms of teachers' guidance in the learning process, and this is informed by their interpretation of learning and cognition.

Elaborating on Bronfenbrenner's theory on the ecology of human development, Cole *et al* (1987) discussed the teacher-child exchange:

> ...it is easy to see such events as 'caused' by higher levels of context; a teacher gives a lesson, which is shaped by the classroom it is a part of, which in turn is shaped by the kind of school it is in, which in turn is shaped by the community and so on. (cited in Cole, 1996:134)

I argue that a teacher's pedagogic strategy is also shaped by her interpretation of educational ideas such as learning and cognition, which in turn is informed by their life histories, in particular their educational experiences, the school cultures they are in, the social environment in which they grew up and the culture in which the social environment is embedded. Any foreign ideas that enter a culture might be assimilated into the indigenous one, or rejected if there is a clash of cultural values – as when the Chinese teachers do not find the new pedagogy beneficial to children's development.

Apparently, in the process of transforming the pedagogy, the teachers also have to achieve equilibrium between theory and practice. When they first experimented with the new pedagogy and found that it was beyond or even clashed with their idea of learning, they bounced back to rely on their previously assimilated educational values and practices. The complexities of this cultural fusion is explained in the following diagram.

Diagram C: Complexities of fusion of Chinese and Western ideas at the two kindergartens

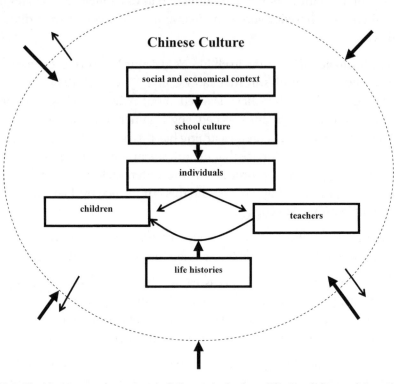

Note: The big arrows represent assimilation and rejection of Western influence into and out of the Chinese culture

Some mainland Chinese teachers argue that the limitations of their approach are due to the constraints they encounter, such as insufficient time or materials. Others reckon that the five thousand years of Chinese history has created today's social atmosphere in mainland China and that traditional education is deeply rooted. It will not be as open, that is westernised, as it is in Macao SAR, so it is difficult if not impossible, for teachers to implement the approach at Girassol. This line of reasoning not only highlights the impact of their own education on the mainland Chinese teachers, but also reminds us that societal and cultural influences on people are profound. These may all be legitimate reasons for the differences in the pedagogical approaches employed and the abilities developed in children in the two kindergartens.

According to Chinese cultural and educational values, as illustrated in these two contexts, learning is not about letting children interact with their environment and construct knowledge from their own explorations and experiences. Children need to participate as agents in learning, whether under continuous guidance or demonstration and imitation, and teachers' role in guiding their learning is still crucial in children's cognitive development. As Cole (1985) suggested, culture and cognition are not separate entities but are inextricably interrelated.

Theme III – Creating a cultural product

Themes I and II reveal the ways in which two different social contexts culturally construct the kindergartens and how each facilitates children's cognitive development in its own ways. Any educational institution should have stated goals and beliefs for children's learning and cognitive development which underpins its pedagogy; however, although the goal may be the same for different schools, there could be different ways of reaching this goal. The current educational goal of both Girassol and Customs Kindergartens is to pursue a creative pedagogical approach. Schools on either side of the Chinese/Macao border are given guidelines by their government, however vague or specific, on how to foster this human capacity in children, and each encounters this challenge with their own school culture and character.

As outlined in Chapter 3, creativity is an educational concept which has not received much attention in the Chinese educational context despite the fact that creativity is seen in so much ancient work in mainland China (Gardner, 1989). Its long tradition in Western countries has made it a Western educational concept even though its importance is not always recognised in the Western educational arena either (*NACCCE Report*, 1999). There is still no consensus on the meaning of creativity in the Western scholarly world, let alone about how it should be fostered. Likewise, Chinese scholars interested in studying this human capacity hold disparate views of this illusive concept. There is general agreement that originality and imagination are the key elements of creativity but the cultural perspective is often neglected (Gardner, 1989).

The educational authorities advise Chinese teachers to foster creativity in children by freeing them from restrictions and encouraging them to ask questions, express their opinions and learn through carrying out tasks by themselves. But these ideas are contrary to traditional Chinese education, where obedience, conformity and collectivism have been the core values in Chinese culture, whether in child rearing or education (Kessen, 1975; Tobin *et al*, 1989; Bai, 2000). Growing up with these Chinese values, teachers are inevitably deeply influenced by them. The current educational reform expects teachers to employ a new pedagogy to teach Chinese children, one that follows Western educational beliefs in cognitive development. How will the old pedagogy be transformed into the new one? In what ways is the new pedagogy transplanted into these Chinese classrooms? Possible answers can be found amongst the practitioners' life histories, the perspectives of creativity and the transformational process observed.

Teachers' interpretations of creativity

According to the teachers' life histories, the notions of fostering creativity in children were encountered for the first time when they were receiving in-service teacher training. Although the local education bureau has informed them as to what the authority thinks creativity is and how to foster it in children, they have arrived at their own interpretation of creativity.

Girassol Kindergarten

As theories about creativity in both Western and Chinese literature suggest, the term means different things to different people. A relatively common understanding amongst the teachers at Girassol Kindergarten is that creativity means making something new and distinctive, either from scratch or by modifying an object to turn it into something else, or having an idea that did not exist before. These responses highlight originality as a key criterion of creativity. This is in line with the general consensus on what creativity is (Xu, 2002). Only the headteacher relies on the official literature and asserts that the elements of creativity entail fluency, originality, flexibility and imagination. The class teachers suggest that creativity means manifesting one's ideas. They associate the term with freedom and the leeway to make choices and use space. They believe it calls for a risk taking personality that dares to try out new ideas and not be afraid to make mistakes. Their interpretation of creativity is in line with the information provided by the education authority, which in turn is informed by Western scholars or by Chinese scholars educated in the West.

The descriptions share similarities with a Piagetian or constructivist pedagogy which advocates that children learn by actively constructing knowledge in their environment. For this to happen requires educators to provide a rich and stimulating but relatively control free environment to allow children construct knowledge and explore ideas in this environment (Athey, 1990). But at the same time the teachers associate creativity with imitation, meticulous observation of one's environment and attention to detail. These elements are mentioned by Chinese scholars such as Dong (1995) and Hui (1999) and Western scholars such as Gardner (1989). My findings reflect that the Chinese class teachers at Girassol Kindergarten are interpreting the meaning of creativity in terms of both Western and Chinese educational ideas at once.

The teachers assume that creativity is an innate ability which needs to be fostered by adults or it will disappear. They imply that to foster creativity, adults have to employ fresh approaches to nurture it, such as the Creative Teaching approach. Under nurturance, children's creativity will be manifested in their work or ideas. This view highlights the importance of social interactions between teachers and children and amongst children, as well as the teachers' guiding role in children's manifestation of creativity. These interpretations of creativity indicate that the teachers at Girassol Kindergarten follow a socio-cultural perspective of children's cognitive development (Anning and Edwards, 1999) in which learning focuses on interactions between adults and children. Since they provide continuous guidance, involving a great deal of discussion with their pupils, the social structure (language), as described by Vygotskian scholars, is also of significance in promoting children's creativity in this context.

Customs Kindergarten

As noted in Theme I, China maintained its monoculture until the 1980s and the teachers' life histories make it clear that they have experienced Chinese traditional education throughout their years of schooling. The term creativity was not heard until after or towards the end of their initial teacher training education, which focused on establishing their techniques and skills. Chinese leaders revived the need for establishing a creative education in the 1990s and discussions and journal articles about fostering creativity flourished. Expectations stated in official documents, such as the Guidelines described here, stem from a Western individualistic culture in which the individual is valued over the group and conformity to other people's ideas is usually despised. However, because they are products of Chinese culture, the teachers at Customs Kindergarten have a specific interpretation of creativity.

Although the teachers are from different parts of China and have slightly different ideas of what creativity means, it appears that there are a few key ideas. Among these are the following: an ability to manipulate with one's hands; newness of an idea, whether new or a modification; an extension of one's thinking based on what they have learned from their teachers. The teachers' responses suggest that to them creativity means refining or extending foundational knowledge or abilities and being able to realise one's ideas by applying technical skills such as meticulous observation, imaginative use of materials, and skills as well as knowledge. Their interpretation of creativity is deeply influenced by Chinese indigenous educational ideas in that they see foundational knowledge and the ability to apply techniques and skills as underpinning creativity.

According to this interpretation children's creativity cannot be developed unless they have been taught the foundational knowledge and skills. Creativity is thus a cultural product and not an innate capacity and teachers play a crucial role in constructing children's creativity.

The mainland Chinese teachers see their role in children's manifestation of creativity and the role of children in developing creativity by practising and applying skills as both being essential. So the social interactions (adult giving something to children) and the agent (child takes on and extends what is being given) combine to construct a cultural product. This is further evidence that the constructivists' and the socio-cultural theory of learning and cognitive development are not mutually exclusive.

Remarkably, even though the teachers have come across Western theories of creativity, their interpretations do not reflect them. They do not recognise the key role of abstract thinking such as imagination, self-expression and individual initiative. Their teaching experiences have persuaded some teachers that the Western theories do not apply to their social context. Theories do not always resonate in teachers' pedagogy but their work experiences and life histories shape their beliefs in

154

the efficacy or usefulness of a theory to a particular social context. A similar phenomenon is observed at Girassol Kindergarten (described in Diagram C).

We can see that despite the fact that teachers from both kindergartens are aware of Western theories of creativity, they interpret it specifically in their social context. They reckon that creativity needs to be fostered by interactions with other people. But whereas teachers at Girassol Kindergarten seem to have taken on board some Western educational ideas, in particular personal aspects and allowing space and freedom for thinking, and have assimilated them into their schema of creativity, teachers at Customs Kindergarten still focus almost exclusively on the concepts of building up children's technical skills and foundational knowledge.

Transforming foreign pedagogy
Girassol Kindergarten
To make the picture more complex, the Girassol teachers are trying to put their ideas of creativity, from whatever source, into practice but only within the framework of their interpretations of children's learning and cognitive development. Their life histories show that they have adapted to several pedagogies since becoming kindergarten teachers in the early 1980s. Their way of teaching has changed from delivering a lesson to a class by traditional one-way transmission and demonstration, which the children imitate, to ending a lesson – which is still one-way – with structured group activities to reinforce what has been learned. Next, they moved from structuring group activities to setting up learning centres in the classroom and organising children to play in these centres after a lesson and finish their assignments. The pedagogical approach can be tracked, as they move from a teacher-centred approach towards a more child-centred one, but the teachers still carefully structured and organised all the learning activities. Two characteristics can be identified in the new pedagogies constructed at each kindergarten.

A hybrid pedagogy rooted in Chinese educational ideas and culture
Before they experimented with the new pedagogy – the Project Approach – lessons were largely teacher-centred. Even during artwork

155

activities, the children were given little choice in what to make and which materials to use. Now the new pedagogy demands that teachers free children from restrictions and standards, allow them to express their ideas, encourage them to ask questions, think about them and experience and explore possible solutions by themselves, and evaluate the results. Children now play a more active role in the teaching and learning process. They are given opportunities to make choices and express their independent thinking in various ways while working on open-ended projects, and learn to appreciate and critique one another's work. That the new pedagogy is still rooted in the Chinese educational values is characterised by the Girassol teachers' meticulous guidance, for instance when making something more realistic through many hints and some persuasion, drawing children's attention to the detail of the items, encouraging them to observe pictures carefully, and praising them for memorising what they have observed.

Intriguingly, the application of the Project Approach at Girassol Kindergarten has affected other parts of the curriculum. The teaching and learning of Chinese characters, was probably the most noticeable shift. Previously, the teachers would decide which and how many Chinese characters children should learn in relation to a theme. Since the new pedagogy, the children often come up with ideas and words during class discussions and the teachers display these Chinese characters in their classroom. They found that because the characters were initiated by the children, they were motivated to learn them and their vocabulary grew rapidly.

So as they tried to implement a new pedagogy which is child-centred and underpinned by Western educational ideas, the teachers at Girassol transformed it into a hybrid pedagogy which synchronises Western and Chinese educational ideas and values. The kind of syncretism observed at Girassol can be attributed to the unique *Luso-Chinês* culture of Macao SAR. Practitioners in this social and cultural context can embrace foreign ideas more naturally. And the less hierarchical system in the city and at the Kindergarten empowered the teachers to reflect on their pedagogy, thus actively contributing to its reform.

Social aspects of the hybrid pedagogy

The teachers scaffold children's learning by asking guiding questions which promote and encourage their thinking, and by helping them to acquire basic technical skills. This pedagogy can be described as scaffolding children through their zone of proximal development, in line with Vygotsky's principle, thus helping them to reach higher levels of ability (1978).

Tobin *et al* (1989) note how group spirit and a sense of collectiveness dominate Chinese child-rearing and educational practices. The priority Girassol Kindergarten teachers give to social interaction is also evident in their encouragement of peer collaboration in the learning activities and their efforts to foster a group spirit amongst children. For instance, the teachers encourage children to work in groups or pairs before and during each construction activity. That peer interaction benefits children's cognitive development has been recognised (Rogoff, 1990). Studies on peer interaction (Forman and Cazden, 1985; Tudge, 1990; Rogoff, 1990) draw on Piaget's 'cognitive conflict', according to which novices experience cognitive conflict when facing a problem together but each from their own perspective. The effort to resolve the discrepancy and reach equilibrium (Rogoff, 1990) promotes the children's cognitive development.

That the benefits derived depend partly on the nature of the partnerships requires further investigation. However, the group of children I observed working on a mansion construction showed clearly how they build on one another's ideas and skills whatever their own ability. In addition, each child takes turns to be the helper and work harmoniously towards a common goal. Gregory (2001) describes this reciprocity of learning during the interaction as a kind of synergy coming into play. She notes that the discrepancies in ability between the partners do not stop them from advancing cognitively. We see this at Girassol Kindergarten: creativity is fostered while the sense of community is valued.

Customs Kindergarten

The mainland Chinese teachers spoke about their general ideas about how to foster creativity in children. Many of these ideas differ from those discussed in either Chinese or Western literature (Craft, 2002; Duffy, 1998). But in their practice their main approach is obviously to build up the foundational knowledge and skills of their pupils, usually through the teacher-directed teaching strategies. This emphasis on imitation resembles the precise instructions and explicit demonstrations given in certain cultures by adults or masters (Lave, 1978; Childs and Greenfield, 1982) and signify a much more teacher-directed pedagogy.

A modified pedagogy rooted in Chinese educational ideas and culture
The teachers at Customs Kindergarten supplement their teaching with giving children opportunities to practise what they have seen modelled by their teachers after the direct teaching. Early childhood educators in mainland China are still debating the effect of demonstrations on children: will creative thinking be jeopardised if the children can copy from adults (Liu, 1999)? Or does imitation precede creative work and set the stage for it (Dong, 1995; Liu, 1997; Ji, 2003)?

The mainland teachers seem to see imitation as creating a platform for cognitive advancement. Their supplementary pedagogy gives children time and some space to try out their ideas after observing teachers' demonstrations and precise instructions. The supplementary pedagogy signifies that the teachers' pedagogy is placing children more centrally in the learning process, but in a particular way. These teachers have transformed the suggested pedagogy by appending the relatively child-centred approach on to the end of their direct teaching instead of blending the two together. This pedagogical strategy is also observed during their music and physical education lessons and story time. Findings from this and other studies (Kessen, 1975; Tobin *et al*, 1989) might explain why the new pedagogy is transformed in this way.

First, the culture and social system in which the teachers reside and function as kindergarten teachers is by and large hierarchical. They are accustomed to following instructions from their superiors. Their life histories reveal that the traditional pedagogy is teacher-centred does not encourage discussion or questioning. Learning is achieved by imitation and repetition. Consequently, it is not surprising that they are unaccustomed to taking risks or trying out anything unfamiliar.

A second point concerns the kind of exposure these teachers have had to other pedagogies and, more importantly, the kind of discussions about the underlying beliefs of each of the possible pedagogies. The physical layout of the classroom is illustrative: the learning centres are added on to the teacher-centred pedagogy. They exist in form but are not fully utilised to promote learning and cognitive development.

Thirdly, Chinese culture on the mainland is so resistant to other cultural practices and ideas that these are bounced off or accommodated on the margins of the culture, while the people default to their old cultural practices. The Taiwanese culture described in Tobin *et al* (1989) and the mainland Chinese teacher's interpretations of creativity revealed in this study support this explanation.

Social aspects of the appendage pedagogy

While a sense of collectiveness and group spirit remains highly valued, the dove-tailing pedagogical approach at Customs Kindergarten encourages individual thinking rather than peer collaboration. When the children have difficulties, all they can do is wait for their teachers to help them. The teachers' praise of the children's behaviour and work draws attention to a model for others and reinforces imitation and competition.

Learning from peers who, by the teachers' standards, are role models has been described in Tobin *et al* (1989) as a strategy employed by the mainland teachers to stimulate children's desire to outperform others. Similarly, the photographs of desirable behaviours in bedroom and classroom areas use the children as role models. This differs from the implications of Piaget's cognitive conflict and also from the peer collaboration theories described earlier. Here, peer influence on children's cognitive development is competition instead of collaborative development. As we can see from examination-oriented education, when opportunity and resources are scarce, the desire to compete is keen.

Paradoxically, according to the Customs practitioners' interpretation, the peer collaboration they see in Girassol is regarded as important for children's learning and cognitive development. While trying to foster children's creativity, Customs teachers have encouraged a sense of individuality and competition amongst the children, thus sacrificing the social aspect of the new pedagogy as they adapt a Western educational idea at the kindergarten.

A non-linear transformational process

Although both kindergartens are contriving to meet the governments' expectations, the teachers' perspectives on children's learning, cognition and creativity inform their teaching. There appears to be a variety of fusions of both Western and Chinese indigenous educational ideas.

The pedagogy at Girassol is becoming increasingly favourable to allowing more space for children to develop in numerous ways while a small part of Chinese educational traditions is retained. In response to the demands of a creative pedagogical approach, the teachers have blended a Western-imported pedagogy into their 'old' pedagogy, syncretising two rather different pedagogies to form their own vision of a creative pedagogy.

At Customs, the indigenous teacher-centred pedagogy still predominates. Influenced by Western educational ideas, the teachers provide some space for the children to develop. Possibly children will be granted more space in their learning in future. Since the teachers' understanding of creativity is deeply rooted in Chinese ideas, their new pedagogy remains teacher-directed, and only a supplementary part of it allows children to apply their own ideas and thinking. In both kindergartens, Western-imported ideas are modified or rejected whenever there is a clash of cultural values and the practitioners resort to the Chinese strategies they are already practising.

The transformational processes of both pedagogies are rather complex and each is specific to the social and cultural contexts in which the kindergartens are embedded. In Macao SAR, the *Luso-Chinês* culture and the teachers' educational background appears more receptive to Western ideas of creativity, which they selectively adapt while preserving, consciously and unconsciously, those valued in Chinese culture. Even though official policy requires teachers to adopt a more liberal pedagogy, these teachers have essentially preserved the indigenous pedagogy, while appending the expected strategy at the peripherery and sacrificing certain Chinese values in pursuit of a creative pedagogical approach.

The various influences operating in any particular culture should not be seen as being in a linear causal relationship; instead each contributes to the social phenomena so formed (Cole, 1996). As Rogoff *et al*

160

(1993) suggested, learning situations are structured according to the practitioner's ideas of education and this is in turn informed by their goal of development, and the values and practices considered important in their culture. This is certainly the case in the two kindergartens examined in this book.

Conclusion

One of the notions of culture is to extend human development as in an artificial environment such as a kindergarten. (Cole, 1996:143)

This book is about the ways in which a pedagogy which is underpinned by Western progressive educational ideas is transformed and implemented to foster creativity in children at two Chinese government kindergartens in Macao SAR and Zhuhai SER China. Some broad questions of concern were: Can educational goals and ideology move across countries and cultures? What happens when we try to transplant Western goals into a country which has different goals, traditions and values? Based on some preliminary information, I have also raised more specific questions, for example: What are the teachers' understandings of learning, cognition and creativity at these kindergartens? In what ways is the pedagogy transplanted into the two kindergartens? What effects do the new pedagogies have on children's development and learning? I attempted to search for answers to these questions by reviewing the relevant literature and collecting information from the two kindergartens. The evidence I collected is grounded in the two kindergartens and the contexts in which they are embedded. The evidence is triangulated in order to project a clearer picture of the social phenomena. In this concluding chapter, I summarise the findings, elaborate on what the local teachers and policy makers can make of the results and discuss the theoretical implications that are revealed by the study.

A summary of the results

Changes in the conceptualisation of educational ideas occur in the social contexts as the teachers in each assimilate various pieces of information from a given idea. Changes are neither automatic nor instant. The participants have helped us realise that as an educational idea moves across countries and cultures, the social, historical and cultural aspects of a society and the life history of the practitioners have a profound impact on their current understanding of children's learning, cognition and creativity.

The children at the kindergartens in Macao SAR and Zhuhai SER grow up in two specific social contexts and develop specific forms of knowledge, abilities and skills, even though the social contexts are within the same Chinese culture. This study argues that, in the course of pursuing a creative programme, both the kindergartens contrive to adapt to a pedagogy which encourages independent thinking and creative art work activities that were not the foci of their curricula and teaching approaches. Consequently, two forms of pedagogical approaches emerge in accordance with the social and cultural characteristics of each city.

According to the interviews conducted and the review of the literature, it appears that there is no objective definition of creativity; rather, it is a culturally-constructed concept. Creativity is interpreted differently in societies that uphold liberal democracy from those that favour less liberal social systems. And the ways used to foster creativity differ accordingly. It is therefore irrelevant to evaluate which way is more effective in fostering creativity in children; rather, the so-called 'effectiveness' should be read in terms of the 'appropriateness' or 'suitability' of an approach within a specific socio-cultural context.

Although creativity is often associated with individuality and independent thinking, within the Chinese context which focuses on uniformity and hierarchy, directive teachers still assume roles in children's learning and cognitive development, including their development of a creative mind. However, in the two Chinese kindergartens which are embedded in two rather diverse social and economic contexts, the extent to which a child is encouraged to think independently or granted opportunities for independent thinking vary according to how teachers assimilate relevant information, how they interpret creativity and the leeway they have in the implementation of their superiors' expectations to foster creativity in children. Underpinning the two transplanted and transformed pedagogical approaches which aim at fostering creative minds, the interplay of socio-cultural influences and children's learning patterns and styles will produce different forms of creativity. The findings of my study suggest that Chinese cultural and educational practices have also influenced the practitioners' pedagogical approach, which in turn creates an impact on their children's cognition. Under the influence of the larger environment, thinking styles differ.

Messages for practitioners
Macao SAR

First, the local education bureau does not intend to supersede traditional education in Macao kindergartens altogether but rather to enrich it with more liberal pedagogical strategies. However, the underpinning beliefs of such strategies and traditional ideas of education are not always compatible. In that case, which part of traditional education should be preserved is unclear. I found that the practitioners' understanding of creativity differs from that described by local government. The practitioners' understanding stems from teaching experiences which have incorporated both Chinese educational ideas and the local education bureau's Western-oriented suggestions to foster creativity in children. The practice in actual settings suggests that children's observation and imitation, which have been a dominant feature of Chinese children's learning, are still valued in today's classrooms and are associated with notions of creativity. The practitioners have shifted from explicit demonstration and instruction to continuous guidance or scaffolding which entail discussion and a more egalitarian status between teachers and learners. These findings raise concerns over which parts of the former pedagogy should be preserved and which modified or abandoned.

Second, there is evidence that although creativity is generally regarded as a Western concept which is underpinned by the ideology of individualism, in the Chinese social and cultural context, peer collaboration and ideas and abilities which emanate from social cohesion are also important in fostering creativity. Hence, the group spirit and sense of community so highly valued in Chinese culture are worth preserving in classrooms instead of pushing for individual uniqueness in the drive to foster creativity. While many countries are learning from programmes that originate in the West and advocate progressive educational ideas, it should be noted that the uniqueness of a culture and its fundamental values should be preserved. It is therefore important for the government to recognise that Western educational ideas are underpinned by Western ideas of individualism while the Chinese educational system is underpinned by a sense of community. There is no simple way to transplant ideas across cultural zones. The significance of cultural preservation and the need for sensible adaptation to Western educational ideas should be acknowledged.

Third, as there is no consensus on what creativity is, whether the abilities that are fostered at Girassol Kindergarten are manifestations of creativity is questionable. But the abilities the children manifest are certainly not the five elements believed by the local education bureau to comprise creativity. For this official definition of creativity, which is based on Western theories on creativity in the 1960s, to become suitable for Chinese teachers and pupils, it might need some modification in order to bridge the gap between educational principles and practices.

Fourth, educational reform should not be a top-down process. It should acknowledge social factors such as the life history and beliefs of the practitioners involved in the reform. Their social and educational background is highly likely to influence their pedagogy and, when taken into account, will help policy makers to adopt a different perspective on the issue.

Fifth, in the actual setting where educational reform takes place, there is strong concern that children, especially those who are passive in learning, may not receive enough attention and guidance from teachers in the acquisition of basic skills and techniques. Their progress in learning and development might slip and therefore cannot catch up with the more active, independent and autonomic children under the kind of liberal pedagogy that has been put into practice. Most educators believe that the right conditions would allow time for open ended activities, a good supply of materials and space and a low child-teacher ratio, and thus reduce the number of children at risk of falling behind the rest.

Sixth, the findings at Macao SAR reveal how teachers are themselves cultural constructions of their social and historical contexts. Their discourses inform their pedagogies and therefore produce specific learners with specific forms of knowledge and ability. Since educational reform is still underway, there is no reason to stop reflecting on what creativity means to people in the Macao community or in what other ways the current curriculum and pedagogy can be modified to explore possibilities and stretch the limits of this cultural concept, going beyond construction activities as the key means to foster creativity in children.

Zhuhai SER

In mainland China, the government prepares a set of guidelines to facilitate the implementation of Quality Education. This has become the framework for education at all levels in China. The document shows that the role of creativity is recognised in contemporary Chinese ideas of education. The interviews indicated that some mainland Chinese kindergarten teachers have an interpretation of creativity, learning and cognition and the pedagogy they currently employ to foster creative minds in children that differs from the official recommendations. As teachers are the implementers of any curriculum, it is necessary for the Chinese government to acknowledge this gap and narrow it.

First, the educational ideas of these mainland practitioners are profoundly influenced by their social and educational experiences as we saw in their discourses on learning and creativity. Yet, the government's expectation of a 'creativity-oriented' pedagogical approach, which prioritises the expression of personality and the uniqueness in how this is manifestated over the standard requirements concerning the acquisition of skills and techniques are not fully implemented. The Chinese ideas of education that underpin the practitioners' discourses and the transformed pedagogy argue for an integration of indigenous educational ideas into the Guidelines before completion of the final version.

Research shows that culture and cognition are not independent entities. While the government associates 'free' expression of ideas and individual forms of manifestation with creativity, the practitioners' strong belief in the role imitation and acquisition of foundational knowledge and skills in the development of children's creativity cannot be ignored. Traditional as it may seem, local practitioners value demonstration and imitation as effective mediations for learning. This is an important signal. The further away we move from historical and traditional practices, the further we are from our own cultural experiences. Rather than forfeiting all the elements in the traditional approach, a combination of traditional and Western pedagogies might work best for Chinese children. Most of the teachers in my study think there should be a balance between obvious demonstration, which signifies a traditional pedagogy in the Chinese and other cultures, and the less explicit teacher guidance observed in relatively child-centred classrooms. This fusion of approaches will hopefully open up opportunities for children to engage in more abstract thinking and imagining, an important element for a creative mind.

Second, these teachers have experienced only the traditional pedagogy, which is characterised by a restrictive atmosphere, one-way transmission of knowledge and demonstration of skills. It is not surprising that they are unfamiliar with a suggested pedagogy that advocates liberating children's learning experiences in less restrictive, more egalitarian and child-centred classrooms. This anomaly needs to be acknowledged and taken into account in any guidelines for a creative programme and pedagogy. The lack of consensus on the meaning of creativity suggests that an operational definition of it is required which takes account of viable Chinese ideas of education also. Such an amalgam could show the way to achieving the Chinese version of creativity.

Third, there is evidence that in this kindergarten peer influence is used to stimulate competition amongst children rather than encouraging a sense of community in the classroom. Some of the children's learning activities are shifting to a more individualised approach. But the importance of group spirit, which is part of Chinese heritage and valued by most participants in my study deserves to be passed on from generation to generation. Moreover, in a country where the One-Child Policy is enforced, the need to social skills through peer collaboration in children cannot be neglected. The significance of reinforcing group spirit should be reaffirmed and emphasised in the Guidelines.

Last but not least, my study shows that there is quite a gap between what the government expects and what actually happens in school settings. This creates a rift between the governments' and headteachers' expectations and the practitioners' view and implementation of a creative pedagogy. Practitioners should have more support, such as establishing a low teacher-child ratio, and a balanced curriculum which allows time for open ended activities. Equally, more channels should also be available to facilitate the exchanges of discourses amongst the different levels in the hierarchical system that characterises mainland educational settings.

The socio-cultural approach exhibited in Chinese kindergartens

Cross-cultural studies on creativity are scant and those carried out in China were done by Western scholars (Gardner, 1989; Cox *et al*, 1999). These studies are either based on general observations or on children's work and performance such as drawings. These researchers have not systematically examined the Chinese teachers' conception of cognition and learning so as to explain their views about creativity and how to foster it in children. As an insider, I have highlighted the social, political and cultural aspects of creativity that can broaden the horizon of cross-cultural studies and deepen our understanding of creativity as an educational concept and a human capacity.

Theories of cognitive development put much emphasis on comparing Piagetian and Vygotskian ideas and increasingly highlighting the social and cultural aspects of children's cognition and learning. Examining the Chinese practitioners' discourses on learning, cognition and particularly their views on creativity, indicates that the Vygotskian or social-cultural theory of cognition is present in Chinese preschool classrooms. The theory can also be applied in the fostering of creativity. I hope this book will generate more ideas about the applicability of the Vygotskian theory in educational settings.

The findings outlined here confirm earlier studies of creativity in that its meaning is contingent upon many factors and there is no ultimate consensus on what these are. They also reveal previously unidentified facets of creativity. First, demonstration and imitation are parts of creativity in the Chinese social-cultural context. Second, in a culture which values a sense of collectiveness, the fostering of creativity is not about displaying individuality but about collective wisdom and a collective sense of learning.

There are debates in the literature about whether imitation hinders or promotes children's learning and cognitive development. Chinese scholars who regard imitation as an important element in children's learning have not presented clearly how these elements enter class-rooms and benefit children's learning. In the two social settings of my study, the role of imitation is found to be subtle. It is applied as a stepping-stone or springboard for children's cognitive advancement. However, the degree and form of advancement that imitation initiates varies in accordance with the teachers' educational ideas and peda-gogic strategies. When a place is increasingly exposed to foreign in-fluences such as more open-ended and child-centred pedagogical approaches, it accepts or remains resilient to those influences accord-ing to its own characteristics and direction for change. But the parti-cipants' perspectives involved in the process – in this case the Chinese teachers – informed by their life and social experiences, can actually determine which influences they will take on or reject. The processes of cultural fusion observed reveal that education is not independent of its social and cultural contexts. The notion of cultural fusion brings out the complexities involved in the transplantation of pedagogical ideas and strategies from one context to another.

In addition, various scholars have suggested the benefits of peers to children's cognitive development. The sense of community or together-ness is nurtured at Chinese kindergartens through routines and activi-ties that draw children together. The group morning exercise is a typical example. Nonetheless, peer collaboration which aims at working towards a common goal socially and cognitively is not common at Cus-toms Kindergarten. While the teachers are endeavouring to foster a creativity which connotes uniqueness and originality of ideas, their approach is to make children work on their own and with only their own ideas instead of letting them work collaboratively with others. Whether children's cognitive development results from cognitive con-flicts, as suggested by Piaget, or by means of social interactions with more-capable partners, as advocated by Vygotsky, or synergised by their equals, when children only work in the presence of others instead of working with them socially and cognitively, the benefits of peer collaboration as described in the literature are likely to be undermined. When the sense of competition in school settings and at home is keen,

170

peer collaboration is simply not possible since each child is the only child in the family. Peer collaboration, then, is no longer a natural phenomenon; rather, it is culturally determined and depends largely on children's social contexts.

Epilogue

This book does not claim to be an authoritative account of the state of Chinese kindergarten education. Rather, it is an investigation of means and approaches to learning which could be systematically presented and implemented. It is important that although this particular study has come to an end, there is further investigation of the transplantation and transformation processes that underscore public and private schools in China which operate disparate practices. Moreover, even though this book has provided some answers to the questions which triggered this investigation, other questions remained to be answered, such as the context-specific conditions and factors which will facilitate the development of creative minds in young children.

The realisation by the two governments of the significance of promoting creativeness in students is a by-product of foreseen competition for economic wealth, power and a sense of security amongst countries as well as persons. While admiring foreign cultures and, in particular, hoping to learn from the West what creative education should be like, it may be more important to look back – at our history and culture – look down – at ground level practice – and even look inside – our lives and needs – for some sensible and viable answers.

I still pay visits to Zhuhai for various purposes and every time I have to walk pass the Gate. For me, it is more than a stone monument. It symbolises part of Chinese history, cultural differences within the same culture and different perspectives. There are many issues yet to be discovered about the two cities.

Bibliography (English)

Anning, A and Edwards, A (1999) *Promoting Children's Learning from Birth to Five.* Buckingham: Open University Press

Athey, C (1990) *Extending Thought in Young Children – a parent-teacher partnership.* London: Paul Chapman

Bai, L (2000) The Chinese Kindergarten Movement. In R. Wollons (ed) *Kindergartens and Cultures.* New Haven: Yale University Press

Baker-Sennett, J, Matusov, E and Rogoff, B (1992) Sociocultural processes of creative planning in children's playcrafting. In P. Light and G. Butterworth (eds) *Context and cognition: ways of learning and knowing.* New Jersey: LEA

Bodrovo, E and Leong, D J (1996) *Tools of the mind.* Ohio: Prentice Hall

Brownell, C A and Carriger, M S (1998) Collaboration among toddler peers: Individual contributions to social contexts. In M. Woodhead, D. Faulkner and K. Littleton (eds) *Cultural worlds of early childhood.* London: Routledge

Brown, A L and Ferrara, R A (1985) Diagnosing zones of proximal development. In J.V. Wertsch (ed) *Culture, communication, and cognition: Vygotskian perspectives.* Cambridge: Cambridge University Press

Bruner, J (1986) *Actual minds, possible worlds.* Massachusetts: Harvard University Press

Chao, R K (1994) Beyond parental control and authoritarian parenting style: Understanding Chinese parenting style through the cultural notion of training. *Child Development* 65(4) p1111-1119

Chard, S C (2000) *Project Approach* (translated Chinese version). Taipei: Kuang Yu Cultural Enterprise Co Ltd

Chard, S C (2001) *Project Approach.* http://www.project-approach.com/definition.htm Accessed in April 2002

Childs, C P and Greenfield, P M (1982) Informal modes of learning and teaching: The case of Zinacenteco weaving. In N. Warren (ed) *Advances in cross-cultural psychology* (vol 2) London: Academic Press

Cole, M (1985) The zone of proximal development: where culture and cognition create each other. In J.V. Wertsch (ed) *Culture, communication and cognition: Vygotskian perspectives.* Cambridge: Cambridge University Press

Cole, M (1990) Cognitive development and formal schooling: the evidence from cross-cultural research. In L. C. Moll (ed) *Vygotsky and education*. Cambridge: Cambridge University Press

Cole, M (1996) *Cultural Psychology – a once and future discipline*. Massachusetts: Harvard University Press

Cole, M (1998) Culture in development. In M. Woodhead, D. Faulkner and K. Littleton (ed) *Cultural worlds of early childhood*. London: Routledge

Cole, M, Griffin, P and The Laboratory of Comparative Human Cognition (1987) *Contextual Factors in Education*. Madison: Wisconsin Centre for Education Research

Cole, M and Scribner, S (1977) *Culture and thought: a psychological introduction*. New York: John Wiley and Sons Inc

Cook, B J (1999) Islamic versus western conceptions of education: reflections on Egypt. In L. King (ed) *Learning, knowledge, and cultural context*. The Netherlands: Kluwer Academic Publishers

Cox, M, Perara, J and Fan, X (1999) Children's drawing in the U.K. and China. *Journal of Art and Design Education* 18(2) p173-181

Craft, A (2002) *Creativity and Early Years Education*. London: Continuum

Csiksentmihalyi, M (1996) *Creativity: flow and the psychology of discovery and invention*. New York: Harper Colins

Dahlberg, G, Moss, P and Pence, A (2000) *Beyond Quality in Early Childhood Education and Care – postmodern perspectives*. Philadelphia: Falmer Press

Daniels, H (2001) *Vygotsky and Pedagogy*. London: Routledge Falmer

Duffy, B (1998) *Supporting Creativity and Imagination in the Early Years*. Buckingham: Open University Press

Edwards, C, Gandini, L and Forman, G (eds) (1998). *The hundred languages of children: the Reggio Emilia approach – advanced reflections*. New Jersey: Ablex Publishing Ltd

Forman, E A and Cazden, C B (1985) Exploring Vygotskian perspectives in education: the cognitve value of peer interaction. In J.V. Wertsch (ed) *Culture, communication, and cognition: Vygotskian perspectives*. Cambridge: Cambridge Unversity Press

Gardner, H (1989) *To Open Minds*. New York: Basic Books

Goodson, I and Sikes, P (2001) *Life History Research in Educational Settings – learning from lives*. Buckingham: Open University Press

Gregory, E (2001) Sisters and brothers as language and literacy teachers: synergy between siblings playing and working together. *Journal of Early Childhood Literacy* 1(3) p301-322

Gregory, E and Williams, A (2000) *City Literacies: learning to read across generations and cultures*. London: Routledge

Hedegaard, M (1990) The zone of proximal development as basis for instruction. In L.C. Moll (ed) *Vygotsky and education: instructional implications, and application of sociohistorical psychology*. Cambridge: Cambridge University Press

Ho, I T (2001) Are Chinese teachers authoritarian? In D.A. Watkins and J.B. Biggs (eds) *Teaching the Chinese learner: psychological and pedagogical perspectives.* Comparative Education Research Centre, The University of Hong Kong

Hudson, L (1966) *Contrary Imaginations.* London: Methuen

Katz, L G and Chard, S C (1998) Issues in selecting topics for projects. http://ericeece.org/pubs/digests/1998/katzpr98.html Accessed in April, 2002.

Kessen, W (1975) *Childhood in China.* New Haven: Yale University Press

Lave, J (1978) Tailored learning: education and cognitive skills among tribal craftsmen in West Africa. Manuscript, University of California, Irvine

Lee, W O (1999) The cultural context for Chinese learners: conceptions of learning in the Confucian tradition. In D. A. Watkins and J. B. Biggs (eds) *The Chinese learner: cultural, psychological, and contextual influences.* Victoria: ACER

Luria, A R (1976) *Cognitive development: its cultural and social foundations.* Massachusetts: Harvard University Press

Macao Special Administrative Region (2002) *Chief Administrator's Annual Policy Address* http://www.gov.mo/policy/en2002_policy.pdf Accessed in April 2007

Macao Special Administrative Region (2003) *Chief Administrator's Annual Policy Address* http://www.gov.mo/policy/en2003_policy.pdf Accessed in April 2007

Macao Special Administrative Region Statistics and Census Service (2006) *Global results of by-census.* http://www.dsec.gov.mo/c_index.html Accessed in April 2007

Malaguzzi, L and Gandini, L (1993) For an education based on relationship. *Young Children* 49(1) p9-13

Maynard, F (1973) *Guiding your child to a more creative life.* New York: Doubleday and Company Inc

Mead, M (1964) *Continuities in Cultural Revolution.* New Haven: Yale University Press

NACCCE Report (1999) *All Our Future: Creativity, Culture and Education.* London: DfES

Nutbrown, C and Abbott, L (2001) Experiencing Reggio Emilia. In L. Abbott and C. Nutbrown (eds) *Experiencing Reggio Emilia: implications for pre-school provision.* London: Open University Press

Rogoff, B (1984) Introduction: thinking and learning in social context. In B. Rogoff and J. Lave (eds) *Everyday cognition: Its development in social context.* Massachusetts: Harvard University Press

Rogoff, B (1990) *Apprenticeship in thinking: cognitive development in social contexts.* Oxford: Oxford University Press

Rogoff, B and Gardner, W (1984) Adult guidance of cognitive development. In B. Rogoff and J. Lave (eds) *Everyday cognition: its development in social context.* Massachusetts: Harvard University Press

Rogoff, B, Mistry, J, Gūncū, A and Mosier, C (1993) Guided Participation in Cultural Activity by Foddlers and Caregivers. *Monographs on the Society for Research in Child Development* Serial No 236, 58(8)

Runco, M A (1996) Personal creativity: definition and developmental issues. *New Directions for Child Development* (72) p3-30

Smith, J A (1996) Semi-structured interviewing and qualitative analysis. In J.A. Smith, R. Harre and L.V. Langenhove (eds) *Rethinking Methods in Psychology.* London: Sage

Spradley, J (1979) *Participant Observation.* Fort Worth: Harcourt College Publishers

Sternberg, R J and Lubart, T I (1995) *Defying the Crowd – cultivating creativity in a culture of conformity.* New York: The Free Press

Stone, C A (1987) What is missing in the metaphor of scaffolding. In D. Faulkner, K. Littleton and M. Woodhead (eds) *Learning relationship in the classroom.* London: Routledge

Tharp, R G and Gallimore, R (1988) *Rousing minds to life: teaching, learning, and schooling in social context.* Massachusetts: Cambridge University Press

Tobin, J, Wu, Y H and Davidson, D (1989) *Preschool in Three Cultures: Japan, China, and the United States.* New Haven: Yale University Press

Triandis, H C (1990) Cross-cultural studies of individualism and collectivism. In J J Berman (ed) *Nebraska Symposium on Motivation: Cross-cultural Perspective. Current Theory and Research in Motivation.* Lincoln, NE: University of Nebraska Press

Tudge, J (1989) When collaboration leads to regression: some negative consequences of socio-cognitive conflict. *European Journal of Social Psychology* (19) p123-138

Tudge, J (1990) Vygotsky, the zone of proximal development, and peer collaboration: implications for classroom practice. In L. C. Moll (ed) *Instructional implications and applications of sociohistorical psychology.* Cambridge: Cambridge University Press

Vygotsky, L S (1978) *Mind in society: the development of higher psychological processes.* Massachusetts: Harvard University Press

Vygotsky, L S (1981) The instrumental method in psychology. In J V Wertsch (ed) *The concept of activity in Soviet psychology.* NY: Sharpe

Wertsch, J V (ed) (1985) *Culture, communication and cognition: Vygotskian perspectives.* Cambridge: Cambridge University Press

Wertsch, J V, Rio, P D and Alvarez, A (1995) *Sociocultural studies of mind.* Cambridge: Cambridge University Press

Whiting, B B and Edwards, C P (1988) *Children of different worlds: the formation of social behaviour.* Massachusetts: Harvard University Press

Winner, E (1989) How can Chinese children draw so well? *Journal of Aesthetic Education* 23(1) p41-63

Wollons, R (2000) *Kindergartens and Cultures – the global diffusion of an idea.* New Haven: Yale University Press

Wong, N C (1999) Preschool Education. In M. Bray and R. Koo (eds) *Education and Society in Hong Kong and Macao: comparative perspectives on continuity and change.* Hong Kong: The Hong Kong University Press

Xu, S (1977) *The Explanations of Characters and Words.* Beijing: Chinese Bookshop

Bibliography (Chinese)

澳門特別行政區教育暨青年局（2002 年）《創思教學》。教師參考資料。
Aomen te bie xing zheng qu jiao yu ji qing nian ju (2000) *Chuang Si Jiao Xue* (Creative Teaching). Jiao Shi Can Kao Zi Liao (Reference Materials for Teachers)

陳幗眉 (1996)。<<學前教育新論>>。北京師範大學出版社。
Chen, G M (1996) *Xue Qian Jiao Yu Xin Lun* (*New Theories for Preschool Education*). . Beijing: Beijing Shi Fan Da Xue Chu Ban She (Beijing Educational Press)

<<辭海>>（1961）。香港: 中華書局辭海編輯所。
Ci Hai (*Sea of Words*) (1961). Hongkong: Zhong Hua Shu Ju Ci Hai Bian Ji Suo (Editing Centre for Dictionaries of China Book Store)

<<辭海>>（1979）。上海辭書出版社。
Ci Hai (*Sea of Words*) (1979). Shanghai: Shanghai Ci Shu Chu Ban She (Shanghai Dictionary Publishing Co)

<<辭源>> (1951)。商務印書馆香港分馆。第 364 頁。
Ci Yuan (*Origin of Words*) (1951). Shang Wu Yin Shu Guan Xiang Gang Fen Guan (The Commercial Press (Hongkong) Ltd)

<<辭源>>（修訂本）1980 年。商務印書館香港分館。
Ci Yuan (*Origin of Words*) (1980). Shang Wu Yin Shu Gua Xiang Gang Fen Guan (The Commercial Press (Hongkong) Ltd)

董奇 (1995)。<<兒童創造力發展心理>>。浙江教育出版社。
Dong, Q (1995) *Er Tong Chuang Zao Li Fa Zhan Xin Li* (*The Developmental Psychology of Children's Creativity*). Zhejiang: Zhejiang Jiao Yu Chu Ban She (Zhejiang Educational Press)

樊玉蓮（2001）。幼兒美術教育中創造性表現能力的培養。*學前教育信息與研究、實踐與探索*。第 4 期, 第 10~11 頁。
Fan, Y L (2001) You er mei shu jiao yu zhong chuang zao xing biao xian neng li de pei yang (Fostering of creativeness in early childhood art education). *Xue Qian Jiao Yu Xin Xi Yu Yan Jiu, Shi Jian Yu Tan Suo* (*Information, Research, Implementation and Exploration of Preschool Education*) (4) p10-11

郭宇澄（2001）。在體育活動中培養幼兒的創造能力。*學前教育研究*。第 4 期, 第 69頁。
Guo, Y C (2001) Zai ti yu huo dong zhong pei yang you er de chuang zao neng li (Foster children's creativity in sports activities) *Xue Qian Jiao Yu Yan Jiu (Preschool Education and Research)* (4) p69

何曉夏（1988）。陳鶴琴論幼稚教育。*學前教育*。第 3 期, 第 80~92 頁。
He, X X (1988) Chen Heqin lun you zhi jiao yu (Chen Heqin talked about early childhood education). *Xue Qian Jiao Yu (Preschool Education)* (3) p80-92

回春茹（1999）。《兒童情商與創造力培養》。中國人民出版社。
Hui, C R (1999) *Er Tong Qing Shang Yu Chuang Zao Li Pei Yang (Fostering Children's Emotional Quotient and Creativity)*. Beijing: Zhongguo Ren Min Chu Ban She (China Ren Min Press)

霍力岩 (1995)。<<學前比較教育學>>。北京師範大學出版社。
Huo, L Y (1995) *Xue Qian Bi Jiao Jiao Yu Xue (Preschool Comparative Education)*. Beijing: Beijing Shi Fan Da Xue Chu Ban She (Beijing Educational Press)

季雲飛（2003）。怎樣看待幼兒的創造性。*早期教育*。第 5 期, 第 19 頁。
Ji, Y F (2003) Zen yang kan dai you er de chuang zao xing (How to consider children's creativeness). *Zao Qi Jiao Yu (Early Years Education)* (5) p19

江海燕 (1999)。<<世紀之交師範教育面臨的挑戰>>。廣州: 新華書店。
Jiang, H Y (1999) *Shi Ji Zhi Jiao Shi Fan Jiao Yu Mian Lin de Tiao Zhan (Challenges of Normal Teacher Education in the Turn of the Century)*. Guangzhou: XinHua Book Shop

教育暨青年局課程改革工作組 (1999 年)。<<幼兒教育及小學預備班 –大綱>>。澳門: 教育暨青年局。
Jiao Yu Ji Qing Nian Ju Ke Cheng Gai Ge Gong Zuo Zu (1999) *You Er Jiao Yu Ji Xiao Xue Yu Bei Ban-Da Gang (Early Childhood Education and Preparatory Class of Primary Education – Guidelines)*. Aomen: Jiao Yu Ji Qing Nian Ju (Macao: Education and Youth Affairs Bureau)

金纓（2001）。對幼兒藝術創造力培養因素的思考。*學前教育信息與研究、實踐與探索*。第 4 期, 第 19 頁。
Jin, Y (2001) Dui you er yi shu chuang zao li pei yang yin su de si kao (Thoughts on factors in the fostering of children's artistic creativity). *Xue Qian Jiao Yu Xin Xi Yu Yan Jiu, Shi Jian Yu Tan Suo (Information, Research, Implementation and Exploration of Preschool Education)*(4) p19

李道佳, 郭曉琴(1997)。 <<幼兒素質教育- 21 世紀人材奠基工程>>。遼寧師範大學
　　出版社。
Li, D J and Guo, X Q (1997) *You Er Su Zhi Jiao Yu – 21 Shi Ji Ren Cai Dian Ji Gong*
Cheng (Quality Early Childhood Education – the fundamental engineering for the
talented in the 21st century). Liaoning: Liaoning Shi Fan Da Xue Chu Ban She (Liaoning Normal University Press)

李桂林, 戚民所及錢萬山 (1995)。 <<中國近代教育史資料匯編>>。北京: 人民教育
　　出版社。
Li, G L, Qi, M S and Qian, W S (1995) *Zhongguo Jin Dai Jiao Yu Shi Zi Liao Hui Bian*
(Edited Information on History of Education of Modern China). Beijing: Ren Min Jiao
Yu Chu Ban She (Ren Min Educational Publishing Co)

李嘉曾 (2000)。 <<創造的魅力>>。江蘇科學技術出版社。
Li, J Z (2000) *Chuang Zao De Mei Li (The Charm of Creation)*. Jiangsu: Jiangsu Ke
Xue Ji Shu Chu Ban She (Jiangsu Science and Technology Press)

劉國權（1999）。影響幼兒創造力發展的幾個教育因素。*幼兒教育*。第 6 期, 第
　　6~7頁。
Liu, G Q (1999) Ying xiang you er chuang zao li fa zhan de ji ge jiao yu yin su (Factors
affecting the development of children's creativity). *You Er Jiao Yu (Early Childhood*
Education) (6) p6-7

劉偉麗（1997）。在做做玩玩中重視幼兒思想創造力的培養。*龍岩師專學報*。第 4
　　期, 第 158~159頁。
Liu, W L (1997) Zai zuo zuo wan wan zhong zhong shi you er si xiang chuang zao li
de pei yang (Fostering children's thinking and creativity in play). *Long Yan Shi Zhuan*
Xue Bao (Journal of Long Yan Normal School) (4) p158-159

劉羨冰 (1999)。 <<澳門教育史>>。 北京: 人民教育出版社。
Liu, X B (1999) *Aomen Jiao Yu Shi (History of Macao Education)*. Beijing: Ren Min Jiao
Yu Chu Ban She (Ren Min Educational Publishing Co)

羅竹風 (1988)（編）。<<漢語大辭典>>。三聯書店（香港）。
Luo, Z F (1988) (ed) *Han Yu Da Ci Dian (Chinese Language Dictionary)*. Hongkong: San
Lian Shu Dian (San Lian Book Store)

羅英智 (1997)。 幼兒素質教育的基本原則。 載於 <<幼兒素質教育 - 21 世紀人材奠
　　基工程>>。李道佳, 郭曉琴 (編)。遼寧師範大學出版社, 第 26-40 頁。
Luo,Y Z (1997) You er su zhi jiao yu de ji ben yuan ze (The Basic Principles of Quality
Early Education). *Zai yu You Er Su Zhi Jiao Yu – 21 shi ji ren cai dian ji gong cheng.(In*
Quality Early Childhood Education – the fundamental engineering for the talented in
the 21st century). D. J. Li and X. Q. Guo (eds) Liaoning: Liaoning Shi Fan Da Xue Chu
Ban She (Liaoning Normal University Press)

潘潔（1993）。<<幼兒教師教育學基礎>>。河南教育出版社。
Pan, J (1993) *You Er Jiao Shi Jiao Yu Xue Ji Chu* (*The Foundations of Education for Early Childhood Education Teachers*). Henan: Henan Jiao Yu Chu Ban She (Henan Educational Press)

彭震球 (1997)。<<創造力教學實踐>>。臺北五國圖書出版社。
Peng, Z Q (1997) *Chuang Zao Li Jiao Xue Shi Jian* (*Implementing the Teaching of Creativity*). Taibei Wu Guo Tu Shu Chu Ban She (*Taipei Wu Guo Books Publishing Co*)

舒新城 (1981)。<<中國近代教育史資料>>。第二版。北京: 人民教育出版社。
Shu, X C (1981) *Zhongguo Jin Dai Jiao Yu Shi Zi Liao* (*Information on History of Education of Modern China*). Di Er Ban (2nd edition). Beijing: Ren Min Jiao Yu Chu Ban She (Ren Min Educational Publishing Co)

舒新城、沈頤、徐元誥、張相 (1947)（主編）。<<辭海>>。香港: 中華書局。
Shu, X C, Shen,Y, Xu, Y G and Zhang, X (1947) (eds) *Ci Hai* (*Sea of Words*). Hongkong: Zhong Hua Shu Ju (China Book Store)

宋青 （2001）。自主性音樂活動促進幼兒創造力發展。*學前教育信息與研究、實踐與探索*。第 4 期, 第 12~14 頁。
Song, Q (2001) Zi zhu xing yin yue huo dong cu jin you er chuang zao li fa zhan (Autonomic musical activities promote the development of children's creativity). *Xue Qian Jiao Yu Xin Xi Yu Yan Jiu. Shi Jian Yu Tan Suo* (*Information, Research, Implementation and Exploration of Preschool Education*) (4) p12-14

桑青松 (2001)。 現代教育理念下的幼兒創新教育思考。 *學前教育研究*。 第四期。 11-13。
Sang, Q S (2001) Xian dai jiao yu ni lian xia de you er chuang xin jia yu si kao (Thinking early childhood creative education under the contemporary educational ideas). *Xue Qian Jiao Yu Yan Jiu* (*Research on Early Childhood Education*) (4) p11-13

佟勳功, 李梅, 李燦明(1997)。 由 '應試教育' 轉變爲素質教育的困難分析及對策研究。 長春社會科學院, *社會科學探索*。 五月, 第 38-46 頁 。
Tong, X G, Li, M and Li, C M (1997) You 'ying shi jiao yu' zhuan bian wei su zhi jiao yu de kun nan fen xi ji dui ce yan jiu (A study on the difficulties and appropriate strategies of the changes from 'examination-oriented' education to quality education). Changchun She Hui Ke Xue Yuan (Changchun College of Social Sciences) *She Hui Ke Xue Tan Suo* (*Exploration of Social Sciences*) Wu Yue (May) p38-46

屠美如(編) (2002)。<<向瑞吉歐學甚麼? - <<兒童一百種語言>>解讀>>。中國: 教育
    科學出版社。
Tu, M R (ed) (2002) *Xiang Rui Ji Ou Xue Shen Mo? – er tong yi bai zhong yu yan jie
du* (*What to Learn from Reggio Emilia – decoding Children's One Hundred Languages*). Beijing: Jiao Yu Ke Xue Chu Ban She (Education and Science Press)

涂豔國 (1998)。 現代教育與幼兒解放。 *華東師範大學, 教育科學版*。 第三期, 第
    23-30頁。
Tu, Y G (1998) Xian dai jiao yu yu you er jie fang (Contemporary Education andl
Liberating Children). Hua Dong Shi Fan Da Xue (The Normal University of East China):
Jiao Yu Ke Xue Ban (*Science of Education Section*) (3) p23-30

王本陸 (2002)。 教學轉型與基礎教育課程改革。 *教育研究*。 第 9 期, 第 67-68
    頁。
Wang, B L (2002) Jiao xue zhuan xing yu ji chu jiao yu ke cheng gai ge (Transforma-;
tion of Pedagogy and Reform for Foundational Education). *Jiao Yu Yan Jiu* (*Educa-!
tional Research*) (9) p67-68

王慧中、顧國強、黃惟珩 (1998)。<<實用創造力及開發教程>>。上海: 同濟大學出版
    社。
Wang, H Z, Gu, G Q and Huang,W H (1998) *Shi Yong Chuang Zao Li Ji Kai Fa Jiao
Cheng* (*Practical Creativity and the Development of Teaching Process*). Shanghai: Tong
Ji Da Xue Chu Ban She (Tong Ji University Press)

吳重光（1993）。《教學心理》。廣東教育出版社。
Wu, C G (1993) *Jiao Xue Xin Lī* (*The Psychology of Teaching*).Guangdong: Guangdong Jiao Yu Chu Ban She (Guangdong Educational Press)

夏征農 (主編)。<<辭海>> (1999)。 上海辭書出版社。
Xia, Z L (ed) (1999) *Ci Hai* (*Sea of Words*). Shanghai: Shanghai Ci Shu Chu Ban She:
(Shanghai Dictionary Publishing Co)

徐立（2002）。創造性教育在呼喚創造型教師。*教師雜誌*。第二期, 第 20~25 頁。
Xu, L (2002) Chuang zao xing jiao yu zai hu huan chuang zao xing jiao shi (Creative
education is calling for creative teachers). *Jiao Shi Za Zhi* (*Teacher's Magazine*) (2)
p20-25

181

楊德廣 (2002)。 樹立新的教育概念, 迎接加入 WTO 的挑戰。 *教育研究*。 第 11 期, 第 32-39頁。
Yang, D Q (2002) Shu li xin se jiao yu gai nian, ying jie WTO de tiao zhan (Establishing new educational concepts, meeting the challenges of joing W.T.O.). *Jiao Yu Yan Jiu (Educational Research)* (11) p32-39

幼兒教育(2001)。 幼兒教育指導綱要(試行)。 9 月號, 第 4-5 頁。
You Er Jiao Yu (*Early Childhood Education*) (2001). You Er Jiao Yu Zhi Dao Gang Yao Shi Xing (The Guidelines for Early Childhood Education – Trial Version) 9 Yue Hao (September) p4-5

袁愛玲（2000）。促進幼兒創造性發展的條件。*幼兒教育*。浙江幼兒師範學校。 四期, 第 158~159 頁。
Yuan, A L (2000) Cu jin you er chuang zao xing fa zhan de tiao jian (Conditions for promoting the development of children's creativeness). Zhejiang You Er Shi Fan Xue Xiao (Zhejian Normal School for Kindergarten Teachers) *You Er Jiao Yu (Early Childhood Education)* (4) p158-159

張麗瓊 (2000）。幼稚園科學教學的創造性教育。*學前教育文薈*。第 2 期, 第 20~21 頁。
Zhang, L Q (2000) You zhi yuan ke xue jiao xue de chuang zao xing jiao yu (Creative education for the teaching of science in kindergartens). *Xue Qian Jiao Yu Wen Hui (Collected Works of Preschool Education)* (2) p20-21

趙承福 (2002)。 對創造教育的幾點認識。 *教育研究*. 第 6 期。 第 35-41頁。
Zhao, C F (2002) Dui chuang xin jiao yu de ji dian ren shi (Some understanding of creative education). *Jiao Yu Yan Jiu (Educational Research)* (6) p35-41

中國學前教育研究會 (1999)。<<中華人民共和國幼兒教育重要文獻匯編>>。 北京 師範大學出版社。
Zhongguo xue qian jiao yu yan jiu hui (Chinese Research Society for Early Childhood Education) (1999) *Zhong Hua Ren Min Gong He Guo You Er Jiao Yu Zhong Yao Wen Xian Hui Bian (Important Documents Edited for Early Childhood Education in the People's Republic of China).* Beijing: Beijing Shi Fan Da Xue Chu Ban She (Beijing Normal University Press)

朱家雄 (2000)。方案教學的理論與實踐。
http://5110.163.com/document/viewxml.asp?d=339 。下載於 2002.12.11。
Zhu, J X (2000) Fang an jiao xue de li lun yu shi jian (The ideology and practice of project approach).http://5110.163.com/document/viewxml.asp?d=339 Accessed in November 2002

朱家雄, 裴小倩 (2003)。維果茨基理論在早期教育中的運用。*幼兒教育*。第二期, 4-7。
Zhu, J X and Pei, X Q (2003) Wei guo ci ji li lun zai zao qi jiao yu zhong de yun yong (Applications of Vygotskian Theories to Early Years Education). *You Er Jiao Yu* (*Early Childhood Education*) (2) p4-7

珠海市教育研究中心 (2001)。《素質教育讀本》（內部資料）。
Zhuhai Shi Jiao Yu Yan Jiu Zhong Xin (2001). *Su Zhi Jiao Yu Du Ben* (*A Book on Quality Education*) (Nei Bu Zi Liao) (Intra-departmental materials)

珠海特區日報 (2001)。珠海市第五次人口普查解讀。B1。
Zhuhai Special Zone Daily (2001) Zhuhai shi di wu ci ren kou pu cha jie du (Decoding the 5th Census of Zhuhai City), B1

Index